The FRIENDSHIP BOOK

of Francis Gay

D.C. THOMSON & CO., LTD.
London Glasgow Manchester Dundee

A Thought
For Each Day
In 1991

Duty makes us do things well, but
love makes us do them beautifully.

Rev. Phillip Brooks.

TUESDAY—JANUARY 1.

THE start of a New Year gives us a clean sheet and an opportunity to make changes.

I would like to pass on, as food for thought, something by the essayist Charles Lamb:

"The man who does not at least propose to himself to be better this year than he was last, must be either very good or very bad indeed."

When David Livingstone offered himself for missionary service, he was asked where he was willing to go.

"I will go anywhere," he said, "so long as it is forward."

A good resolution indeed.

WEDNESDAY—JANUARY 2.

THE Lady of the House and I visited our old friend Mary shortly after her new press-button telephone had been installed. She was still puzzled and ill at ease with it.

"I wish I hadn't been persuaded to have this model," she said. "I was used to my old one and I can't get on with these new-fangled contranklements!"

We sympathised with Mary because we have often felt the same way about new things, but we explained how to use the different buttons and assured her that after she had used her phone for a while she would be happier with it.

On the way home though, we couldn't resist having a chuckle because we thought "contranklements" a lovely new word and one that would fit the bill in our household on many occasions!

THURSDAY—JANUARY 3.

WHEN last year dawned I thought
I would do such a lot of good,
And had not time slipped by so fast
I really think I should.

Now a brave new year is here,
So while it still is new,
I'll do some of those kindnesses
I meant last year to do.

FRIDAY—JANUARY 4.

"CONFIDENCE is generally all the magic needed to work miracles," someone said recently.

Is that true? The trouble is that many of us, at some time or other, lose confidence in ourselves and our abilities. How can we re-acquire it?

One way is to draw up a "balance sheet". Make a list of your successes. You'll be surprised how many there are when you write them down. On another sheet of paper write your "assets" — not financial ones, but such things as good health, the ability to see the humorous side of events and similar qualities.

Study these two papers every day for a fortnight, looking out for confidence boosters, and then write them down, too.

The American poet and essayist Oliver Wendell Holmes said: "The great thing in the world is not so much where we stand, as to what direction we are moving". Daphne du Maurier wrote, "All through life you go through every sort of phase. What's wrong now may well turn out right later on".

Above all, let us live a day at a time. Each day we should try to crush some of those weeds of negative thought that can sap our confidence. It grows stronger with their destruction.

SATURDAY—JANUARY 5.

OUR old friend Mary had been appreciating an unusually mild spell one January and was thankful that she was able to get out to the shops and to economise a little on her heating bills. However, when we called to see her she was feeling a little put out because her milkman had gloomily remarked that "we're bound to suffer for this later on."

"Never mind, Mary," said the Lady of the House comfortingly, "I'm sure you're the one with the right attitude. After all, the milkman isn't in charge of the weather, and what point is there in worrying about what might never happen?"

"You're quite right," replied Mary as we waved her goodbye. "And what's more, the shortest visit from a cheerful person is worth more than any amount of time spent with a grumbler!"

SUNDAY—JANUARY 6.

BLESSED be the God and Father of our Lord Jesus Christ, who hath blessed us with all spiritual blessings in heavenly places in Christ.

Ephesians 1:3.

MONDAY—JANUARY 7.

JOHN NEWTON was a slave trader who was converted to Christianity and became the Vicar of Olney in Buckinghamshire. One day a parishioner asked him what he hoped to find in Heaven.

"If I ever reach Heaven," Newton replied, "I expect to find three wonders. First, to meet some people I had not thought to see there; secondly, to miss some I had expected to see there; and lastly, the greatest wonder of all, to find myself there!"

PEAK PERFORMANCE

TUESDAY—JANUARY 8.

SCHOOL reports are feared and revered by parents and children alike. Some teachers are moved to considerable praise regarding the glowing prospects of certain pupils, while others prefer to be more restrained, knowing that sometimes an apparently dull pupil has hidden abilities that will not blossom until later in life.

One prophecy penned years ago certainly proved correct. It came from John Tate, the second headmaster of Richmond's ancient Grammar School in North Yorkshire, and concerned the son of a clergyman. He wrote:

"I do not hesitate to express my opinion that he possesses, along with other and excellent natural endowments, a very un-common share of genius."

He went on to expand his opinions, but added:

"You must not entrust your son with a full knowledge of his superiority over other boys. Let him discover this as he proceeds . . ."

The lad did indeed make a name for himself — two names, in fact! One was his own, Charles L. Dodgson, the clergyman don and author of weighty mathematical books; the other, Lewis Carroll, the pseudonym he used for his world-famous children's classics, "Alice In Wonderland" and "Alice Through The Looking-Glass".

WEDNESDAY—JANUARY 9.

YOUNG Billy was quite topical with his latest riddle. "Do you know what happened to the thief who stole a calendar, Mr Gay?"

"No, Billy," I replied. "What *did* happen to the thief who stole a calendar?"

"He got 12 months!"

THURSDAY—JANUARY 10.

A FRIEND makes a hobby of collecting unusual shop signs such as the butcher whose signboard proclaimed, "Pleased to 'meat' you", the footwear shop which called itself a "Shoetique" and the hairdresser's called "Snippers".

These are all good, but his prize for ingenuity goes to an antique shop in the little village of Idle which called itself "The Idle Curiosity Shop"!

FRIDAY—JANUARY 11.

HAZEL AITKEN has the knack of saying something worthwhile in just a few lines. Here is an example:

I had to stay in bed awhile,
And time passed rather slow
Until I thought of all the things
That gave my life a glow:
My kindly man and children dear,
A fund of memories, too,
Shared joys and tears, such precious years,
Remembering, time just flew!

SATURDAY—JANUARY 12.

MANY books have been written, many lectures given and sermons preached about worry and anxiety, and how to overcome these feelings which afflict most of us at some time or other.

But amid all the millions of words of advice given I wonder whether any get so near to the point as the simple assertion of the late Dr W.E. Sangster, the well-known Methodist preacher: "If I trust, I do not worry; if I worry, I do not trust."

HELPING HANDS

I've borrowed a few of your rollers, Mum,
To see what can be done;
For why should I have all the curls
While Jennifer has none?

A

SUNDAY—JANUARY 13.

THE Lord is my shepherd; I shall not want. He maketh me to lie down in green pastures: He leadeth me beside the still waters. Psalms 23: 1-2.
(Authorised Version)

MONDAY—JANUARY 14.

RECENTLY, I was looking through the autograph album I kept when I was a schoolboy and I came across an entry written by my uncle:

Think!
And Thank!

I can still remember the disappointment I felt at seeing he had written such a short piece, but as I grew older I came to realise what a lot of good sense there was in those three words.

There are so many ordinary things we can enjoy but are inclined to take for granted — family and friends, loved pets, books, music, the radio and so on. Thinking about them usually leads us to be grateful for them — and that can't be bad!

TUESDAY—JANUARY 15.

IT'S quite easy to convince ourselves that we are poor, even when we know that, in comparison with many others, we are rich in this world's goods. I heard of a schoolgirl in an expensive independent school who wrote in an essay: "Everyone in my house is poor. My father is poor, my mother is poor, my sisters are poor, my brother is poor, the butler is poor, the maid is poor and the chauffeur is poor."

Sometimes I think that we are all a little like that poor little rich girl!

WEDNESDAY—JANUARY 16.

DR WILLIAM BARCLAY once told a story about a church in Glasgow at which he sometimes preached and where the organist was blind.

One morning, the minister announced that the next hymn would be number 216, "For those we love within the veil." "No," said the organist quietly, "that's not 216, but 218."

When Dr Barclay spoke to him afterwards, he was amazed to find that the organist carried in his memory the number of every hymn in the book as well as the whole order of service. He was very humble about his wonderful memory and regarded it as a gift from God to compensate for his loss of sight.

What a lovely example of counting blessings rather than dwelling on misfortunes!

THURSDAY—JANUARY 17.

LUCY LARCOM wrote this poem, "A Strip Of Blue", many years ago. It's a refreshing antidote to many of today's attitudes of materialism and "keeping up with the Joneses".

I do not own an inch of land,
But all I see is mine:
The orchards and the mowing-fields
The lawns and gardens fine.
The winds my tax-collectors are,
They bring me tithes divine,
Wild scents and subtle essences,
A tribute rare and free;
And more magnificent than all,
My window keeps for me
A glimpse of blue immensity,
A little strip of sea.

FRIDAY—JANUARY 18.

I HAVE often felt that the well-known Beatitudes given by our Lord could have embraced another couplet: "Blessed are the encouragers, for they shall be encouraged."

After all, every one of us needs a spot of encouragement at some time. Encouragement has been described as "oxygen to the soul". The patriarch Job was told by his friend Eliphaz that "your words have kept men on their feet".

It doesn't need much. Just a word of appreciation, of thanks, of cheer, can do so much to help a struggler on his way. It was Charles Dickens who once observed that "No one is useless in this world who lightens the burden of it for anyone else".

SATURDAY—JANUARY 19.

A FRIEND had made a mistake which was gently pointed out to her. "Thanks," she said. "I never make the same mistake twice," then added with a smile, "I always make a different one, for the sake of variety."

She had taken the criticism in the right spirit. We all make mistakes and should try to learn from them.

One old gentleman believes in "weighing up" what he hears, then deciding whether the criticism is justified or not.

While an American psychologist, speaking on conquering the fear of making mistakes, advised, "Think positive instead of negative. Bring to mind the times you have succeeded. This will make you realise that life consists of success and mistakes."

Robert Browning surely put it best of all:

We fall to rise, are baffled to fight better,
Sleep to wake.

SUNDAY—JANUARY 20.

HAVE I not commanded thee? Be strong and of good courage; be not afraid, neither be thou dismayed: whithersoever thou goest. Joshua 1:9.

MONDAY—JANUARY 21.

LIFE is full of surprises as we are all constantly finding out.

A minister friend had recently taken over a new church, and he set out to make some pastoral visits. As he walked up a garden path, he was met by a friendly dog which wagged its tail and accompanied him to the door. When the door was opened to admit the minister, the dog went in, too, and ran upstairs.

After a cup of tea and a chat, the minister was ready to go on his way again. At the open door the householder said, "Don't forget your dog, will you?"

"*My* dog!" exclaimed the minister. "I thought he was yours . . !"

TUESDAY—JANUARY 22.

I CAN'T tell you who wrote it, but there is a lot of wisdom packed into this verse:

If a child lives with tolerance,
She learns to be patient;
If a child lives with encouragement,
He learns to have confidence;
If a child lives with fairness,
She learns to show justice;
If a child lives with security,
He learns to have faith.
He or she will learn to find
LOVE IN THE WORLD.

THE GLORY OF STONE

WEDNESDAY—JANUARY 23.

"WHAT a good afternoon we've had!" said the Lady of the House when she returned from the Ladies' Fellowship.

"Our speaker didn't turn up and we were all wondering what we should do, when one of the members suggested we all spoke for a minute or two on something we felt particularly thankful for today. Everybody contributed, even poor Mrs Powell who has had so much to worry about lately. I think many of us came away feeling very humble and with a completely new outlook on life."

Talking about things we have to be thankful for . . . What a good idea! It would be lovely if it spread.

THURSDAY—JANUARY 24.

I WONDER if you know the story of the king who had four sons. He sent the eldest to see a certain fruit tree in Winter, the second to see it in Spring, the third in Summer, and the fourth in Autumn.

Then he summoned them to his presence and asked each to give a description of the tree.

"Just a black ugly skeleton," said the eldest.

"It was beautiful — covered in blossom," said the second.

"Very pleasant in its shady Summer attire of green leaf," said the third.

"Well, I didn't see it like that," said the youngest. "I saw it as a tree filled with delicious fruit."

The king smiled. "There is a lesson to be learned from your answers. You need to know a fruit tree at least a year before knowing what it is truly like — and you need to know a lot about things and people before reaching conclusions about them."

FRIDAY—JANUARY 25.

I WAS delivering leaflets for our church recently and was struck by the variety of letterboxes I encountered. Some were part of a new door, smart and shiny with a brush-like draught-excluding device inside, some had been there since the house was built, some were too high for comfort, some too low, while others had such a stiff spring that I felt lucky not to lose my fingers! Some, of course, were just at the right level, simple to operate, and they made my task much easier.

Outward appearances are not the most important thing, but sometimes first impressions are, and those letterboxes made me think about how other people see us. Are we friendly and easy to approach, or stand-offish, inclined to snap and difficult to get on with, like some letterboxes? I know which I want to be.

SATURDAY—JANUARY 26.

PEOPLE worship God in different ways and with different ceremonies, but underneath the differences there is something which gives us a sense of togetherness. The Indian Christian, Sundar Singh, once expressed this in a striking way when he was asked about the best way of worshipping God.

"In the East, men take off their shoes when they worship God; in the West, they take off their hats; but worshipping God depends neither on shoes nor hats, neither feet nor heads, but on hearts."

SUNDAY—JANUARY 27.

AND immediately he received his sight, and followed him, glorifying God: and all the people, when they saw it gave praise unto God. Luke 18:43.

MONDAY—JANUARY 28.

I AM sure that at some time you must have heard authors, actors, or musicians asked, "How do you react to the critics — do you pay heed to them or not?" I have heard various answers to the question; some people will not read critical appraisals because they find them too upsetting, and I have even heard some say that they would hide in a corner rather than read what the critics said about their work.

The actor, Sir Michael Hordern, takes a very different view: "Oh, I love the critics," he says. "They have taught me such a lot over the years, and I often adopt the suggestions that they make."

Surely this is how it should be? We should all be ready to listen to criticism, and, where it is true and useful, act upon it.

TUESDAY—JANUARY 29.

LIFE is made
of ifs and buts,
of maybes
and perhapses,
of rushing forward,
falling back,
progressions and
relapses.

But don't get worried
if you find
you're losing steps,
and paces —
for though today
you lag behind,
tomorrow you'll win
races!

Anne Kreer.

WEDNESDAY—JANUARY 30.

HAVE you heard the story from Denmark about the fox and the stork?

The fox disliked the stork and decided to play a trick on her. He invited her to a meal and brought the soup to the table in a bowl that was so shallow that the stork, with her long bill, was unable to eat it.

The stork realised that she had been tricked, so the next day she invited the fox to share a meal with her, and she served the soup in a tall, narrow jug so that the fox could manage only a lick or two. Then the fox realised that if only he had treated the stork kindly in the first place, she would have probably returned *his* kindness.

An old saying reminds us that "one good turn deserves another". The wise Earl of Chesterfield is noted as saying, "Do as you would be done by is the surest method I know of pleasing". While Charles Kingsley, author of "The Water Babies" wrote: "The loveliest fairy in the world; and her name is Mrs Doasyouwouldbedoneby".

THURSDAY—JANUARY 31.

A COUPLE of neighbours of ours took their four-year-old grandson to the Zoo and then to a restaurant for lunch. Grandad felt for his new bifocal spectacles to read the menu — and found that they were missing.

"I know where they are," piped up little Joel. "They're at the Zoo. When you lifted me up to see the bears, they fell out of your pocket."

Trying hard to keep calm, Grandad asked, "Joel, if you saw them fall, why didn't you tell me?"

"Well," replied the little boy, "after you stepped on them, I thought you wouldn't want them any more."

FEBRUARY

FRIDAY—FEBRUARY 1.

ROSEMARY has long been associated with remembrance, and even in ancient Greek and Roman times it was thought that it improved the memory. In the Middle Ages, it was a popular herb for medicines, cooking and for warding off the plague. It was also used for decorating churches at Christmas until eventually holly took its place.

Shakespeare immortalised it with poor, mad Ophelia saying to her brother, "There's rosemary, that's for remembrance; pray, love, remember", and until this century it was customary for a sprig of rosemary to be carried at a funeral as a symbol that the departed one would not be forgotten.

According to legend the flower was once white, but when the Virgin Mary took flight into Egypt with Joseph and Baby Jesus, her cloak passed over a rosemary bush. Its colour was transferred to the flowers which have remained blue ever since.

SATURDAY—FEBRUARY 2.

I CAME across these anonymous lines recently. I'm passing them on because they express something many of us have discovered to be true:

If only all the world could learn
The simple art of living;
They'd know that each was born to fill
His daily life in giving.
For only those who love to give
Have ever really learned to live!

SUNDAY—FEBRUARY 3.

GRACE be to you and peace from God our Father, and from the Lord Jesus Christ.

Corinthians II 1:2.

MONDAY—FEBRUARY 4.

I COULDN'T live without books. They give so much lasting pleasure, they become like old friends. Obviously, Dorothy Wordsworth shared the same sentiments. This is an extract from a letter she wrote to the poet Coleridge:

"Yes . . . send me a book, a beautiful book, peculiar, distinctive, individual; a book that hath first caught your eye and then pleased your fancy, written by an author all right out of his heart."

The American author, Mark Twain, felt the same. "A good book," he said, "is the best of friends, the same today and for ever."

TUESDAY—FEBRUARY 5.

A GREAT Italian lawyer, Francesco Carnelutti, was once asked the secret of his success.

"My wife," he replied at once. "She never studied law, does not meddle in my work, and never asks for or gives me advice. But she fills my life with her presence. She anticipates my wishes, guesses my moods, listens to my outbursts, always finds the right word. In the evening, while I am consulting my papers, she sits by me knitting, without saying a word. The noise of the needles is the best tranquilliser I know. It breaks the tension and gives me an infinite sense of security. Without her I would be at a loss. With her I feel I can do anything."

It's a tribute to wives the world over.

WHITE MORNING

WEDNESDAY—FEBRUARY 6.

I WAS in the garden recently when I heard, then saw, a flock of migrating geese flying overhead in their distinctive formation. I suppose it is now instinctive for ducks and geese to fly in this way, but when exactly did they discover that by flying together, an upward lift is created for the bird that follows? Likewise, when did they learn that when all the birds do their part, the whole flock has at least a seventy per cent. greater flying range than if each bird were to fly alone? Not only do they know all this, but it is so strongly instilled in them that should one bird begin to lag behind or drop out of formation, the others call it into position with honks of encouragement.

It suddenly struck me how true this is of life, whether in the fellowship of the Christian Church or of any other faith or cause. It is certainly far easier to live the dedicated life "flying with the flock" than trying to go it alone. I reckon it's good to be called back into position when *we* are tempted to stray, too!

THURSDAY—FEBRUARY 7.

UNTIL the sky is brighter,
until the storm is through,
We've got to make
the best of things —
The best that we
can do.

Until the sky is bluer,
and clouds are free from rain,
let Hope be your umbrella,
until we smile
again.

Anne Kreer.

FRIDAY—FEBRUARY 8.

"MR HAWKER, our vicar, is slightly cracked, but he is a very clever old soul," wrote a young governess in her diary many years ago.

At that time Miss Kucznski, governess to a family in Morwenstow in Cornwall, never imagined that she would marry the "slightly cracked, very clever old soul". But, in fact, she became the second Mrs Hawker when he was 60 years old!

Nowadays when anyone remembers the Rev. Robert Stephen Hawker it is mainly because he initiated the first harvest Festival in October 1843 in his little church with the words:

"Let us gather together in the chancel of our church on the first Sunday of the next month, and there receive the bread of the new corn, that blessed sacrament which was ordained to strengthen and refresh our souls. Let us remember that, as a multitude of grains of wheat are mingled into one loaf, so we, being many, are intended to be joined together into one, in that Holy Sacrament of the Church of Jesus Christ."

Hawker was not always serious. In fact, his love of fun and mischief landed him in many scrapes. So did his generosity, for whenever he heard of anyone in need he hastened to help and indeed, so unsparingly did he help others that he often had to deny himself material comforts. His was the type of compulsive generosity which did not count the cost.

SATURDAY—FEBRUARY 9.

I RATHER like this anonymous comment: "One minute of keeping your mouth shut is worth an hour of explanation."

It bears thinking about, doesn't it?

SUNDAY—FEBRUARY 10.

AND they said, Believe on the Lord Jesus Christ, and thou shalt be saved, and thy house.

Acts 16:31.

MONDAY—FEBRUARY 11.

KENNETH has always been hard of hearing and many a time at school he missed something important. Then he made a new friend, John, who couldn't see very well, and had great difficulty in making out anything on the blackboard. They sat together in class and John used to repeat or write anything the teacher said that his friend hadn't been able to hear, while Kenneth would write out the words on the blackboard that John couldn't read.

John is now a lawyer, and Kenneth a librarian, so neither of them allowed their handicaps to interfere with their progress. Both knew what it was to fight against a handicap, and both succeeded by helping each other.

TUESDAY—FEBRUARY 12.

THEY lived not only in the past,
There are hundreds of thousands still;
The world is bright with the joyous saints
Who love to do Jesus's will.

You can meet them in school, or in lanes or at sea,
In church, or in trains, or in shops, or at tea,
For the saints of God are just like me,
And I mean to be one, too.

I like these lines written by Lesbia Scott. They're a reminder that there are still saints in the world today, all around us and often in the most unexpected places!

WEDNESDAY—FEBRUARY 13.

THE Editor of a local newspaper received a letter from a man in America asking help to find his brother whom he hadn't heard from for over 30 years. Eventually, the Editor managed to track down the missing man and sent a young reporter to tell him that his brother in America would like to hear from him.

"What did he say?" asked the Editor when the reporter returned.

"He thanked us very much for going to so much trouble."

"He'll be going to write to America, then?" asked the Editor.

"Oh, no," said the reporter. "He told me it was his brother's turn to write."

Just a silly story, you may say. But doesn't it remind us of the way in which so often the knowledge that you and I are right holds us back from doing what we ought to do and, in our heart of hearts, would really *like* to do?

THURSDAY—FEBRUARY 14.

PHYLLIS, who lives in Aberdare, sent me these six lines entitled "A Short Course in Human Relations". They say more than a score of books on the subject:

The six most important words: *"I admit I made a mistake."*

The five most important words: *"You did a good job."*

The four most important words: *"What is your opinion?"*

The three most important words: *"If you please."*

The two most important words: *"Thank you."*

The least important word: *"I"*.

FRIDAY—FEBRUARY 15.

DURING World War II, Sir Malcolm Sargent was just about to begin conducting a concert when the air raid sirens sounded.

"Anyone who wishes to leave may do so now," he announced. "The orchestra will carry on. We may be killed, but we shall play something Hitler can never kill."

Not one person left the hall.

Thank God for all the indestructible and beautiful things which no man can destroy.

SATURDAY—FEBRUARY 16.

THE Lady of the House and I have recently enjoyed entertaining some friends from Canada and learning about life over there. Amongst other things, they told us about their Grow a Row scheme.

They had found that one packet of seeds grew far more vegetables than they could use themselves, so, hating good things to be wasted, they decided to "plant a row for others", and encouraged all their friends to do the same. Each week, the surplus was gathered and taken to a deprived part of their city, where anybody in need could have a basket of the lovely fresh produce.

In everyone's community there is someone who would be glad of a freshly-picked lettuce, a little pot of home-made jam or a few small cakes still warm from the oven. If we have something to share, let's pass it on!

SUNDAY—FEBRUARY 17.

AND thou shalt love the Lord thy God with all thine heart, and with all thy soul, and with all thy might.

Deuteronomy 6:5.

MONDAY—FEBRUARY 18.

A CLERGYMAN whose parish is in a farming area, decided to base his Sunday morning sermon on dairy farming and our dependence on milk and dairy products. He used this as an introduction to the theme of his sermon — our need to give and receive the milk of human kindness.

He must have been rather long-winded, I'm afraid, because afterwards someone remarked, "Thank you for the sermon, Vicar, but I think it would have been better had it been condensed!"

TUESDAY—FEBRUARY 19.

EVELYN WOODLEY sent me these four lines which tell, simply but clearly, how we should all build our lives:

Belief — is the start of foundations;
Faith — is the making of strong walls;
Hope — is the roof that covers all;
Love — is the door we enter by.

WEDNESDAY—FEBRUARY 20.

I DON'T know the author of this poem, but it's surely a good lesson for everyday life:

Said the robin to the sparrow,
"I should really like to know
Why these anxious human beings
Rush about and worry so."

Said the sparrow to the robin,
"Friend, I think that it must be
That they have no heavenly Father
Such as cares for you and me."

THURSDAY—FEBRUARY 21.

ON wintry evenings the Lady of the House and I sometimes settle down to enjoy a good TV programme. Some time ago, we watched an interview with the two Bishops of Liverpool, the Roman Catholic Derek Warlock and the Anglican David Sheppard. These two close friends talked of their work to bring harmony to Liverpool and their efforts to solve the many problems of unemployment and hardship in the city.

After the programme, the Lady of the House looked thoughtful. "Francis," she said, "don't you think it is significant that the cathedrals are situated one at each end of Hope Street in Liverpool? After all, when you have an immense problem you need hard work and vision, but it's not going to get you far unless you have the hope that carries you through to the end."

I agreed wholeheartedly with her. Here's to living on Hope Street!

FRIDAY—FEBRUARY 22.

OUR friend Mary was browsing through her old autograph album one day when we went to visit her.

"I like this one, Francis," she said and read out a verse attributed to a poet, Carlotta Perry:

It was only a glad "Good morning"
As he passed along the way,
But it spread the morning's glory
Over the livelong day.

Let's see if we can "spread the morning's glory" over today. It's so easy!

GOLD AND GREEN

SATURDAY—FEBRUARY 23.

CATHERINE BRAMWELL BOOTH, daughter of the founder of the Salvation Army, had some lovely things to say about growing old and the prospect of Heaven. The two I particularly liked are:

"I *don't* want to go, but when I do I shall enjoy it! When one thinks of flowers and trees and the stars and all the wonderful things God has created for *this* world, just *think* what he must have created for eternity!"

"And, of course, butterflies. No wonder old people get wrinkled up like cocoons. Just think what they are going to turn into!"

SUNDAY—FEBRUARY 24.

GRACE be to you and peace from God the Father, and from our Lord Jesus Christ. Galatians 1:3.

MONDAY—FEBRUARY 25.

I STAYED in a village once where the library van called every Thursday afternoon. All the locals used to gather to exchange books — and the latest news, too.

Mrs Harvey, who was in her eighties, borrowed at least three books every week. When I asked her what kind of book she preferred, she told me that she chose ones to suit her moods.

"I take poetry for quiet company, who-dunnits to keep me guessing, love stories to remind me of my youth, and a biography when I want to feel close to someone."

Though widowed and living on her own, Mrs Harvey was never lonely — her books kept her company.

TUESDAY—FEBRUARY 26.

HAVE you heard the story of the Sunday School teacher who was telling her class about the Pharisee in the Temple and how he thanked God because he was so good and not sinful like the publican?

"It is wrong to be self-righteous," she said. "Now children, let us all thank God that we are not like that Pharisee . . ."

WEDNESDAY—FEBRUARY 27.

I LIKE to keep a tidy house,
I like to keep it clean,
But not so very tidy
That ne'er a book is seen,
And not so very spotless
That no-one dare come in,
For what's the use of a palace
If there's no warmth within?

Phyllis Ellison.

THURSDAY—FEBRUARY 28.

A YOUNG man in a steamer sailing down the Mississippi River asked the pilot, "How long have you been navigating on this river?"

"Twenty-five years," was the answer, "and I came up and down these waters many times before that."

"Then," said his passenger, "I should think you will know every rock and every sandbank in the river?"

The pilot smiled. "Oh, no, I don't. But I know where the deep water is — we want to know the safe course, and keep to it."

It's the same in life.

FRIDAY—MARCH 1.

TODAY all over the world, women will be meeting in groups large and small for the annual Women's World Day of Prayer. Barriers of country and denomination are put aside as Christians join together to share in a service with a theme that has been arranged for them by their sisters in perhaps America, Australia or the West Indies.

Traditionally, the final hymn is "The day thou gavest, Lord, is over", which was written by the Rev. John Ellerton more than a century ago. The beautiful words remind us that:

The sun that bids us rest is waking
Our Brethren 'neath the western sky.

With its theme of worldwide Christian fellowship, it is not surprising that it has become so important in the World Day of Prayer — nor that Queen Victoria chose it for her own Diamond Jubilee celebrations.

So, as the ladies lead the way on this first Friday in March, let's try to remember the many things that *unite* the nations of the world.

SATURDAY—MARCH 2.

A FRIEND who listens regularly to a "Thought For The Day" programme on the radio keeps a little notebook in which she jots down from time to time items which have particularly impressed or helped her. She sometimes passes these on to me.

Here is one worth remembering: "A man who is wrapped up in himself makes a very small parcel!"

SUNDAY—MARCH 3.

FOR I know that my redeemer liveth, and that he shall stand at the latter day upon the earth.

Job 19:25.

MONDAY—MARCH 4.

FEELING uncertain? Doubtful of what the future holds? These lines by Dorothy M. Loughran are chosen specially for you:

As a candle's cheerful light
Scatters all the gloom of night,
Hope will come a-shining through,
Lighting up the way for you.

Glowing through the darkest days
Sending out its healing rays,
Beaming like a leading light
Until once more the way is bright.

TUESDAY—MARCH 5.

NICHOLAS HERMAN of Lorraine was clumsy. He had been a soldier, and later, he took a job in a monastery kitchen in Paris. Although he did his best, he always seemed to be breaking things.

He was there for 15 years and as time went by, he became less of a liability. Indeed he was so gentle and considerate that his colleagues grew to love him greatly. Eventually, they wrote a little book called "The Practice of the Presence of God". It reflected the experiences and thoughts in a monastery kitchen of one who had vowed to honour God whether he was at work or at prayer, or indeed, wherever he was.

He became known as the saintly Brother Lawrence.

WEDNESDAY—MARCH 6.

THIS charming poem, "The Troubled Heart", is by Margaret H. Dixon:

My heart, why do you worry so,
While violets peep and March winds blow?
Why should you worry, for no fret
Has ever solved a problem yet?

To cross a bridge before it comes
Is only done by foolish ones,
So take life's steps, one at a time,
My heart — oh, foolish heart of mine.

Learn lessons from the flowers and trees,
Which grow with gentle grace and ease,
Seek only God's sweet Will to do,
And He, my heart, shall guide you through.

THURSDAY—MARCH 7.

I LIKE the old story of a Welsh girl who came to London to work as a maid in one of the big houses. Every Sunday she travelled many miles across the city to worship with a congregation of Welsh speakers. The whole service was conducted in the Welsh tongue.

The family with whom she lived were very kind to her, and invited her to worship with them at their local church. However, the girl very courteously refused, saying that she would rather make the journey to worship in the language which she knew and loved.

The master of the house smiled, and very gently pointed out that Jesus was not a Welshman.

The girl quietly replied, "I know that, sir, but it is in Welsh that He speaks to me."

FRIDAY—MARCH 8.

MONICA DICKENS, whose books have given so much pleasure, tells us she was 60 when she made a great discovery. It was just this: that it's a waste of time trying to make other people the way you think they ought to be. If people are annoying you, it's not because they are annoying, but that you are letting yourself be annoyed.

That may sound complicated, but when I thought it over I knew just what she meant. It's not worth trying to change other people — we ought, instead, to change ourselves to become more tolerant. Then *we* won't annoy other people either!

SATURDAY—MARCH 9.

IN religious art the pelican has long been a symbol of self-sacrifice. The reason for this is that the bird's huge beak looks as if it has been dipped in red dye. This gave rise to the legend that when a mother pelican cannot find food for her young, she thrusts her beak into her breast and nourishes them with her own blood.

All mothers make sacrifices for their children and it is right that they should be remembered with gratitude for their love, care and self-sacrifice, not only on Mothering Sunday, but throughout the year.

As George Herbert, the 17th century poet and hymn writer, so aptly put it: "A good mother is worth a hundred schoolmasters."

SUNDAY—MARCH 10.

HE answereth and saith unto them, He that hath two coats, let him impart to him that hath none; and he that hath meat, let him do likewise. Luke 3:11.

MONDAY—MARCH 11.

HOW do I know that my youth is all spent?
Well, my get-up-and-go has got up and went.

These words were written many years ago by a Mrs Winesain at the age of 90. She didn't write in any attitude of self-pity for she went on to describe with humour the many things she had enjoyed in her long life.

Some people do have a feeling of regret when they are growing old and can no longer do the things they used to. But there are compensations, too — the pleasure of being able to turn over in bed again on a cold morning, time to devote to hobbies old and new, plus the wisdom learned from a long experience of life.

Yes, even when the get-up-and-go has lessened, there's still a lot to be thankful for.

TUESDAY—MARCH 12.

UNDER a Buckinghamshire country road near the Oxfordshire border runs a little tunnel opened in March 1987 — one of the first toad tunnels in the United Kingdom.

Every Spring, thousands of toads emerging from hibernation in the woods fringing the main road from Marlow to Henley-on-Thames had been run over and killed as they made their way to their spawning ponds on the other side of the road.

The Fauna and Flora Preservation Society initiated the building of the little tunnel, and its engineers proudly treasure their certificates recognising that each had "successfully completed a course in the ancient and noble art of toad tunnel construction".

It is estimated that over 90 per cent. of the local toad population now get to the other side of the road in safety.

WEDNESDAY—MARCH 13.

MY dictionary defines a friend as "one loving or attached to another, an intimate acquaintance or a well-wisher". In this poem, "What I Call A Friend", an unknown author describes what he means by friendship:

One whose grip is a little tighter,
One whose smile is a little brighter,
One whose deeds are a little whiter,
That's what I call a friend.

One who'll lend as quick as borrow,
One who's the same today as tomorrow,
One who'll share my joy and sorrow,
That's what I call a friend.

One whose thoughts are a little cleaner,
One whose mind is a little keener,
One who avoids those things that are meaner,
That's what I call a friend.

THURSDAY—MARCH 14.

A LOCAL Methodist congregation had been looking forward to their visit from the Chairman of the District, but unfortunately he was suddenly taken ill, and a local preacher had to take his place.

At the start of his sermon, he said, "I'm a poor substitute — like a piece of cardboard you put over a hole when a window breaks."

Afterwards, he was thanked by one of the members of the congregation, who said, "There was no need to apologise. You weren't a bit of cardboard — you were a real pane!"

A compliment, or an insult? You know, I'm not quite sure!

FRIDAY—MARCH 15.

WHEN I looked in to see our friend John, I found him in the garden hanging out the washing.

"Muriel's a bit off colour," he explained. And then, "How does that look?" he asked, as he pegged the last shirt on the line.

"Fine," I said. "But why do you ask?"

"Well," John replied, "there's more to hanging out washing than meets the eye. Muriel explained that the right place to peg a shirt is at the bottom of the seam. Did you know that, Francis?"

I had to admit I didn't.

"Well," said John, "when you think of it, there's a knack and an art in doing everything. And it makes all the difference."

He's right, you know.

SATURDAY—MARCH 16.

CLARA BARTON, founder of the American Red Cross was once reminded by a friend of an especially cruel thing someone had done to her.

"Don't you remember it?" said the friend.

Clara Barton shook her head. "No," she replied and then added with a smile, "I distinctly remember forgetting it."

How wise! I remember an old lady saying, "If you have a sore place on your body — don't prod it, and if you have injured feelings — leave them alone and let them heal."

SUNDAY—MARCH 17.

FOR whosoever shall do the will of my Father which is in heaven, the same is my brother, and sister, and mother. Matthew 12:50.

MONDAY—MARCH 18.

THE two days of Equinox, March 18th and September 25th, with their 12 hours of both day and night, are very special to me.

The Spring Equinox brings a promise of long days, beautiful flower-filled gardens and walks in the sun.

The Autumn Equinox heralds the days of golden-hued trees, crisp frosty mornings, roaring fires, shopping for relatives and friends, all culminating in the festival of Christmas.

After January and February are over, the slowly lengthening days and the gradual awakening of plants and flowers tell us that another year has begun and that Winter days are over.

Yes, many things change, but the year's round goes on, the seasons come and go and we can but marvel at it all.

TUESDAY—MARCH 19.

I'VE been reading that we are living longer nowadays. Far more people are reaching their eighties and nineties, and in Britain there are now nine times as many centenarians as there were 30 years ago.

So how do we grow old gracefully? The religious writer G. E. Diggle suggests that we "start young" by cultivating interests that we can continue in retirement — gardening, handicrafts, getting involved in organisations that help other people — in fact, anything that helps us to be outward-looking.

What I liked most, though, was this thought:

"While you've a contribution to make, never say 'I've done my share. Now I'm leaving it to the young'. Remember that the young person's contribution is energy, and the older person's is experience."

NATURE'S TREASURES

If we learn to treat with care
All lovely things that grow,
Nurture and watch over them,
Then surely we will know

The purest pleasure to be had,
'Twill stay forever ours,
For time is never wasted
When it's spent among the flowers.

WEDNESDAY—MARCH 20.

IT'S the easiest thing in the world to take things for granted, whether it be the milk delivered to our doorstep each day, clean water running from our taps and light at the touch of a switch — or the loving care we receive from our nearest and dearest. The sad thing is that we often don't appreciate how lucky we are until it's too late.

I am reminded of the young man who, wanting independence, left home and went to share a flat with friends. It wasn't long before he was home again one weekend with a large bag of dirty laundry. As his mother patiently tackled it, he talked at length about the cost of rent and heating, and all the cooking and cleaning that took up so much of his time.

Mother looked sympathetic and said she knew just how he felt. "Oh, it's all right for you, Mum," the young man replied. "You live at home!"

THURSDAY—MARCH 21.

TODAY is the 21st of March, and whatever the weather may be like, it is officially the first day of Spring, so we may look forward to longer days and new life appearing everywhere. Eleanor Farjeon described the innocence and promise of Spring very beautifully in these lines from her "Prayer For Little Things":

Please God, take care of little things,
The fledglings that have not their wings,
Till they are big enough to fly
And stretch their wings across the sky.
Take care of small new lambs that bleat,
Small foals that totter on their feet,
And all small creatures ever known
Till they are strong to stand alone.

FRIDAY—MARCH 22.

SHE was a new helper in the retirement home, well-meaning and anxious to do her best, but, oh, how very nearly she put the cat among the pigeons!

It was all because she thought the residents were being a bit too cliquey.

"Don't you think it would be nice to move to different tables now and then?" she suggested brightly one lunchtime.

There was an appalled silence. Then Mrs Mackie said gently, "No, lass. Our table groups are like little families. We'll stay as we are, thank you."

The helper learned a lesson from that. She realised that the old folk were not being unfriendly when they always sat in the same places. Most of them had lost their own immediate family, or were separated from them by distance; their little groups, sharing each meal together, were like new families to them.

SATURDAY—MARCH 23.

AS our thoughts turn to life, death and resurrection this Easter, these words by Evelyn Woodley hold comfort for us all:

When we die
We lose time,
But gain
Eternity.

SUNDAY—MARCH 24.

BUT to us there is but one God, the father, of whom are all things, and we in him; and one Lord Jesus Christ, by whom are all things, and we by him.
Corinthians I 8:6.

MONDAY—MARCH 25.

I'M sure every housewife will recognise the truth of this humorous poem by D. J. Morris:

If ever the house is all tidy,
As clean and as neat as a pin,
With mountains of food in the cupboard,
Then never a soul drops in.
But say that I start some Spring-cleaning
And there's clutter all over the floor,
I'll bet you a pound to a penny
There's always a knock at the door!

TUESDAY—MARCH 26.

IN a broadcast, Lord Tonypandy, former Speaker of the House of Commons was talking about his Welsh childhood. His family were poor, but his mother always used to say, "If a door is ajar, push it open."

He said he had tried to follow that advice all his life, and had always profited by it. After his retirement as Speaker, he devoted most of his time to helping people less fortunate than himself, especially through causes connected with children's welfare. Through this work he hoped to open doors of opportunity for deprived youngsters.

There is another well-known saying: "As one door shuts, another opens."

The truth of that, too, depends on finding the other door, and realising the opportunities that lie behind it — nowadays, more people are finding such openings to use their talents and experiences and to learn how to work in new directions. Sometimes this occurs after redundancy or retirement, proving that "helpful doors" do indeed exist if we look for them and push them open.

WEDNESDAY—MARCH 27.

"WHAT a lot of evil there is in the world," I overheard someone sigh. Well, I suppose there is, but have you noticed how, where there is evil, there is always goodness, too? Italy gave us the Mafia — and Leonardo da Vinci; Ireland gave us the IRA — and St Columba; Poland gave us the Warsaw Ghetto — and Chopin; America gave us Al Capone — and Abraham Lincoln; Scotland gave us the Massacre of Glencoe — and Alexander Graham Bell.

I'm sure you can think of lots more examples yourself. Even in the darkest days of Nazi rule in Germany and the occupied countries, there were brave souls holding aloft the torch of freedom and Christian courage.

And remember, goodness won in the end — it always does.

THURSDAY—MARCH 28.

HERE is how the Canadian poet Alice Christianson welcomes the arrival of Spring in Ontario:

Sing a song of Springtime,
Of blossom-laden trees,
Of buttercups and daisies,
And butterflies and bees.

Sing a song of Springtime,
Of sudden April showers,
Of robin's nests and rainbows,
And happy, carefree hours.

Sing a song of Springtime,
Of kites with paper wings,
Of skipping ropes and roller-skates,
And roundabouts and swings.

WORKING TOGETHER

Old-fashioned ways
Are often best;
Through centuries
They've stood the test.

Steady does it,
Sure and slow;
Teamwork helps
To make it so.

FRIDAY—MARCH 29.

ONE Good Friday, little Emma was taking part in a Sunday School presentation of the scene preceding the Crucifixion. Emma was one of the crowd who had to cry out, "Crucify Him! Crucify Him!"

She thought how unfair that was. Jesus was the Friend of little children, and she just wasn't going to be a party to crucifying Him, she decided.

The Sunday afterwards, she was telling her Grandma all about it, and Grandma said, "Well, if you didn't cry 'Crucify!' with the others, what *did* you say?"

"I sang, 'For He's a Jolly Good Fellow'," said Emma proudly.

SATURDAY—MARCH 30.

A FRIEND sends me the following meditation which formed the "Thought For The Week" on his church's service paper recently:

"If I can come to the day when there is no-one in the world I hate, no-one I want to steal a march on, no-one I want to spite or put in his place, no victory I want to win over others, but only victories with and for others, surely Lord, in that moment I shall have entered your kingdom."

Difficult? Yes; but then whoever said building a new and better world would be easy? At least, we can try.

SUNDAY—MARCH 31.

JESUS said unto her, I am the resurrection, and the life: he that believeth in me, though he were dead, yet shall he live.

John 11:25.

APRIL

MONDAY—APRIL 1.

IT used to be a popular custom to have a house blessed when people first moved in, perhaps not unlike that of a mother going to church as soon as possible after the birth of her baby for the old ceremony of "churching".

This lovely prayer is a Jewish blessing on a home:

We ask His blessing on this home and all who live in it.
May its doors be open to those in need,
And its rooms be filled with kindness.
May love dwell within its walls,
And joy shine from its windows.
May His peace protect it and His presence never leave it.

TUESDAY—APRIL 2.

WHEN life is bright and all around is fair,
With love, and hope, and beauty everywhere,
How easy then to keep faith bright and clear,
To sing and say, "What need is there to fear?"

But when the road is rough, and winds are keen,
Think of the little bird who sings unseen
In darkness, and bravely sing, trusting still;
Courage and hope shine bright when all is ill.

These inspiring lines were written by Mabel Jeeves who was an invalid for many years, confined to bed and often in great pain. Throughout her illness she continued to write verses and prose pieces to comfort and encourage others in sickness or trouble.

WEDNESDAY—APRIL 3.

RECENTLY a young friend of mine was invited to join a local cycling club. At the time he confided that he was a bit apprehensive, fearing that the standard might be too high for him. However, he was told that the next Saturday run was to be a new members' day, so he plucked up courage and went along.

I met him a few days later and asked how he got on. He was full of enthusiasm. "It was so well organised," he explained. "We were paired off, each new member with an experienced member and it was only when we got to a steep hill that I felt qualms. I was sure it was going to prove beyond me."

"What happened?" I asked.

"Well, we new members were given a helping hand. My partner placed a hand on the back of my saddle, and helped me up the hill — and so I was able to make it to the top."

It's marvellous what a helping hand can do, isn't it?

THURSDAY—APRIL 4.

ALL her life, Barbara Jemison's mother kept an album in which she wrote verses and thoughts which appealed to her. Here is one Mrs Jemison sent to me recently and which I gladly pass on:

A pathway lies before you
Like a tract of forest snow,
Be careful how you tread it
For every mark will show.
And when life's journey's ended
And the pathway you have trod
May your name in gold be printed
On the road that leads to God.

FRIDAY—APRIL 5.

THE other day I saw an open Bible displayed in an optician's window. At first I thought it was there to test the eyesight of those who enjoy doing a bit of window shopping. Next to the Bible, however, was a card with the text, "When life is blurred, God's word is as good as glasses".

I found out that the optician was a lay reader in the local church who never misses the opportunity to combine his two occupations. A far-sighted idea!

SATURDAY—APRIL 6.

SEVEN-YEAR-OLD Andrew Mellor was at home on a mission station in Rhodesia with his sister Deborah, when a knock came at their door. On the threshold stood a group of black soldiers.

The children smiled and asked if their visitors would like some tea. While they were drinking it, Andrew and Deborah chatted happily with them in the Shona language. They had no idea that the soldiers had come to destroy the mission and the white missionaries responsible for it.

However, the Shona people have a proverb, "If I have given you food — and you have eaten — we are friends".

Thus, when the soldiers had finished, they politely said goodbye to Andrew and Deborah and left the mission in peace.

SUNDAY—APRIL 7.

AND it shall come to pass in the last days, that the mountain of the Lord's house shall be established in the top of the mountains, and shall be exalted above the hills; and all nations shall flow into it. Isaiah 2:2.

MONDAY—APRIL 8.

THESE inspiring lines are by the poet George MacDonald:

Take up thy song with woods and trees,
Whilst thou hast heart and living yields delight.
Let that expire, let thy delight in living die —
Then take thy song from field and sky
And join the silent choir.

TUESDAY—APRIL 9.

WE were just about to park the car in a vacant space when suddenly the Lady of the House shouted, "Stop!" We'd nearly run over a teddy bear! Now we were faced with a problem — should we leave it propped up on a fence, hoping its young owner would come back? It was beginning to rain. Should we take it to the police station then, or would the police think we were wasting their time with trivial matters? The young owner wouldn't think it trivial, I was sure of that.

So we went to the police station, and Teddy was taken into custody and duly entered in the lost property book. "Come back next week and I'll let you know if he's been claimed," smiled the desk sergeant, his fingers gently smoothing Teddy's red bow.

I hoped the parents of Teddy's owner would turn to the police in their predicament — I couldn't stop thinking of the grieving youngster whose beloved toy had gone. Well, I'm glad I can report a happy ending — the Teddy who had been taken into custody was later given back into the tender, loving care of his rightful owner.

All right, the main aim of our police is to fight crime and apprehend criminals, but isn't it good to know they still have time to care for a teddy bear, too?

WEDNESDAY—APRIL 10.

I WAS intrigued when I read about "Don't Worry Park". It's in Nanjing in China and is so named because of a lady who lived there hundreds of years ago. She had been born into a very poor family, but the man she married was very rich. When she died, she left the park for the use of ordinary people as a place where they could enjoy peace, beauty and tranquillity.

You and I may not possess great wealth that can be of benefit to others, but each of us has the opportunity to leave behind our own equally-important memorial.

I quote Stephen Grellet's well-known words: "I expect to pass through this world but once; any good thing therefore that I can do, or any kindness that I can show to any fellow creature, let me do it now; let me not defer or neglect it, for I shall not pass this way again".

THURSDAY—APRIL 11.

IT'S not too hard to be honest when we know we're being watched, but suppose you were playing in a big golf tournament, with the chance of making many thousands of pounds. Quite by accident, when you're preparing to hit the ball, you move it just an inch.

You know that nobody saw you, but you know, too, that, to obey the rules, you should add a penalty stroke to your score for that accidental inch.

It would be tempting, wouldn't it? Yet, how you would hate yourself if you didn't do the right thing. The prize money would be like ashes in your mouth.

Only a victory honestly won is a victory worth having.

REFLECTIONS

Never build a fortress
And then withdraw inside,
Loath, perhaps, to face the world
Wrapped in stubborn pride.

Never seek the shadows,
Look instead to light,
The world is full of colour,
Life is joyful, bright.

Old and new together
Can each their bounty share.
Never shrink away from
Building castles in the air.

FRIDAY—APRIL 12.

WHEN George Thomas, Viscount Tonypandy, was Vice-President of the Methodist Conference many years ago, he visited Georgia in the USA, where, as the preacher, he was the only white person in the church.

He has never forgotten the welcome given by the minister, who said: "We are greatly honoured tonight to welcome Mr George Thomas, a British Member of Parliament, who is also a Methodist like us. His face is white, but his heart is as black as ours!"

SATURDAY—APRIL 13.

ONE of the nicest things I know is the sense of optimism that many elderly people are able to inspire in others. An example that comes to mind is the world-famous cellist, Pablo Casals, who never lost his sense of wonder at the happiness that crowded into his life.

He wrote, "For the past 80 years I have started each day in the same manner. I go to the piano and I play two preludes and fugues by Bach. It is a sort of benediction on the house and fills me with awareness of the wonder of life. I have the feeling of the incredible marvel of being alive and human. The music is never the same to me. Each day it is something new and unbelievable. Each day I am re-born."

Inspiring words indeed.

SUNDAY—APRIL 14.

IN thee, O Lord, do I put my trust; let me never be ashamed; deliver me in thy righteousness.

Psalms 31:1.

MONDAY—APRIL 15.

I THOUGHT that this charming little poem from Anne Kreer was ideal for today, the day when the Lady of the House, like so many other housewives, tackles the weekly wash:

It'll all come out in the wash,
and no doubt the day will be fine,
and our worries and cares
will just blow away there,
and dry themselves out
on the line!

TUESDAY—APRIL 16.

RECENTLY, I was writing a difficult letter, trying to comfort an old friend in his bereavement. The right words were hard to find.

Then the Lady of the House called, "Francis, come to the front window! I've never seen a sunset like it."

I'm afraid I didn't welcome the interruption. You know how it is. When you're busy and not getting on very well, it's difficult to welcome a break in your train of thought.

But of course I answered the summons. And how right she was!

It had rained all afternoon. Now the day was ending in a blaze of glory and the western sky was a riot of orange, gold and red, gilding the edges of the clouds, giving the distant hills the light that doesn't seem to be of this world.

We stood together in silence for a few minutes. Then I thanked the Lady of the House and went back to my letter.

You won't be surprised when I tell you that the words I had been seeking for so long now flowed freely.

WEDNESDAY—APRIL 17.

WHEN a friend falls upon bad times, should we sympathise with him or her? According to a counsellor-trained friend of mine, Beth Jackson, the answer should be no!

Beth uses the analogy of someone who has accidentally fallen into a trench and can't get out. The sympathetic person climbs into the trench, sits by the victim and cries real tears with him. The genuine helper stands with one foot on the upper ground and with tender loving care assists the unfortunate person to safety.

Thus, sympathy can be passive, merely a mental or emotional share in a friend's problems, whereas an active means of attempting to remedy the situation is what is needed. We shouldn't *just* provide a listening ear, but commit ourselves to resolving the problem.

In future, when I feel sympathy for another person, I'll endeavour to make it *active* sympathy. As the old saying goes, "A little help is worth a lot of pity".

THURSDAY—APRIL 18.

IT used to be common for children to learn long passages of poetry by heart. Years ago when I was at school, one such familiar piece was Thomas Hood's "I Remember, I remember" with its closing lines:

But now 'tis little joy
To know I'm farther off from heaven
Than when I was a boy.

These words came back to me vividly the other Sunday in church when our service paper had this as the "thought for the week": "If you feel farther from God than once you did, don't be under any illusion as to who it is who has moved!"

FRIDAY—APRIL 19.

"ARE you good at riddles, Mr Gay?" my friend young Billy asked me.

"Yes, fairly good," I replied.

"Well, what comes before seven?"

"That's easy," I said. "Six, of course!"

"Wrong," chuckled Billy. "It's the milkman!"

SATURDAY—APRIL 20.

MY dictionary defines tolerance as a willingness to allow people to hold and express their own opinions — to be themselves, in fact, quite the opposite of that unattractive quality, bigotry.

I am reminded of one of the characters in "Lark Rise to Candleford", Flora Thompson's book about village life years ago. In it, her devout Methodist uncle, "when he heard the sound of the Angelus bell borne on the wind from the Roman Catholic chapel in the next village, would take off his hat and after a moment's silence murmur, 'In my Father's house are many mansions'."

There's an old verse that expresses a similar thought, that each of us is unique, put on this earth to fulfil God's purpose:

To each is given a bag of tools,
An hourglass and a book of rules;
And each must build, ere his time be flown,
A stumbling block or a stepping stone.

SUNDAY—APRIL 21.

AND Jesus went about all Galilee, teaching in their synagogues, and preaching the gospel of the kingdom, and healing all manner of sickness and all manner of disease among the people. Matthew 4:23.

FISHY TALE

I'll have to go back and tell my Dad
That things have changed since he was a lad.
He spins such yarns of fish he caught
Not yards away from this same spot.
Only one I've seen all day,
A whopper — but it got away!

MONDAY—APRIL 22.

RECENTLY, while going through some of my old college notes, I was reminded of my personal tutor who was elderly when I was in my early twenties.

His main subject was Philosophy, and he had a wonderful gift of being able to breathe life and meaning into words from centuries ago.

Occasionally, during lectures, he would turn a saying round and then add a little homespun philosophy of his own. One particular piece of wisdom stuck in my mind:

"All quarrels are destructive, but most of them can be avoided with a smile and an apology — and it doesn't matter who's been in the wrong."

The words then seemed to have little meaning, but on many occasions since, in times of conflict, I've found that a smile and a turning of the other cheek can work wonders.

TUESDAY—APRIL 23.

WHEN the Lady of the House and I were on holiday in Staffordshire, we visited a museum that was also a working pottery. For a long time we watched, fascinated, as the potter flung a lump of clay onto his wheel and gradually drew it up into the shape of a vase. Sometimes he was not satisfied with the result, and once the whole thing collapsed. He simply scooped up the clay to use it again.

It's rather like life — trouble comes along, we make mistakes, our world collapses around us and we may feel tempted to give up. But it's worth remembering that no situation is permanent, life goes on, and something good can be made out of the worst of experiences.

WEDNESDAY—APRIL 24.

FRIENDS and friendship are at the same time the most demanding and the most rewarding things in life.

The poet Longfellow said, "Friendship is better than gold and precious stones", while William Penn tells us, "There can be no friendship where there is no freedom. Friendship loves a free air and will not be penned up in straight and narrow enclosures."

An old Eastern proverb gives us this reminder, "Hast thou a friend? Visit him often, for thorns and brushwood obstruct the road which no one treads."

The saying I like most of all, though, is by Ralph Waldo Emerson: "I awoke this morning with devout thanksgiving for my friends, the old and the new."

With that I cannot, nor would I wish to disagree.

THURSDAY—APRIL 25.

THIS prayer is said to have been found in Chester Cathedral:

Give me a good digestion, Lord,
And also something to digest.
Give me a healthy body, Lord,
And sense to keep it at its best.
Give me a healthy mind, good Lord,
To keep the good and pure in sight,
That, seeing sin, is not appalled,
But finds a way to set it right.
Give me a mind that is not bored,
That does not whimper overmuch
About that fussy thing called "I".
Give me a sense of humour, Lord,
Give me the grace to see a joke,
To get some happiness from life,
And pass it on to other folk.

PEACEFUL PATH

When Spring comes whispering on the breeze
And stirs to life the ancient trees,
What joy to take a leisured walk
With loved ones near and time to talk;

Time to wander through a wood,
In harmony with changing mood,
And ever, as we linger there,
Thank God who made it ours to share.

FRIDAY—APRIL 26.

THE Royal Family pay state visits to many countries where they are often welcomed in quaint ways. An observer recollects that the biggest smile he ever saw on the face of Prince Philip occurred when he and the Queen visited Nepal in 1961.

Not content with a banner declaring "God Save The Queen", the loyal subjects of Katmandu wanted to greet her husband, too. So there was a second banner, which read, "And God Help The Consort"!

SATURDAY—APRIL 27.

THE kingfisher is one of our most beautiful birds. Usually all we see of it is a flash of turquoise and orange as it skims up and down a stream. It is said that originally it was a grey bird, but when Noah released it from the Ark to search for land, it flew so high that it took some of the blue from the sky and it scorched its breast feathers by flying too close to the sun. Noah was angry at the bird's disobedience and wouldn't allow it back into the Ark, so it had to perch on the roof and fly over the water searching for food, as it still does.

Another name for the kingfisher is halcyon, and it was once believed that mating birds made a nest on the sea which always remained calm during the hatching period — hence the term "halcyon days" which we apply to times of peace and calm and happiness.

SUNDAY—APRIL 28.

EVERY good gift and every perfect gift is from above, and cometh down from the Father of lights, with whom is no variableness, neither shadow of turning.

James 1:17.

MONDAY—APRIL 29.

SOME words of advice from the Winchester poet, Dorothy M. Loughran:

Beyond the hill
We cannot see,
Till we have climbed
Its stony way,
Nor unlock doors
Without a key,
Nor journey faster
than today.

So pause awhile,
And leave each day
Its own bright pattern
To unfold,
Each precious thread
Along Life's way —
The bronze, the silver,
And the gold.

TUESDAY—APRIL 30.

I WAS watching a gardening programme on television recently and had been admiring the beautiful flowers. At the end the presenter remarked, "If your plants, whether they have been tucked into a crevice or seeded naturally, look happy, then that's the sign of a really successful garden."

It made me think about the importance of "fitting in" properly in our own situation. There's nothing better than a united family, work that leaves us feeling satisfied, and a hobby that provides pleasure and relaxation. Perhaps we should all aim at being a "round peg in a round hole"! I'm sure we'd all feel so much better for it.

MAY

WEDNESDAY—MAY 1.

IT was many years ago and I had a decision to make which could affect my whole life. Now, when I have a problem I like to get away to a quiet place, and think. In this case, I went to our local park.

I sat down on a bench, and looked up at the tall trees, their branches towering above me. That was when I saw the squirrel — jumping from one high branch to another. At one point, he appeared to be aiming for a limb so far out of reach that his leap looked like suicide. He missed — I gasped — but he landed, safely and unconcerned, on a branch several feet lower. Then he climbed upwards to his goal and all was well.

An elderly man sitting at the other end of the bench said, "Funny, I've seen dozens of them jump like that. A lot of them miss, but I've never seen one coming to any harm." Then he chuckled. "I suppose they've just got to risk it if they don't want to spend their lives on the same branch!"

That's it, I thought — a squirrel has to take a chance when scaling the heights every day. Should I not do the same? My decision was made; and time was to prove that it was the right one. Since then, I have often said thank you to one of God's small creatures.

THURSDAY—MAY 2.

I LIKE the story of the young boy who demanded of his mother, "Do up my anorak!"

"What's the magic word?" asked his mother.

"There isn't a magic word," replied her son. "You just have to fiddle with the zip until it clicks."

FRIENDS ALONG THE WAY

FRIDAY—MAY 3.

AT Aylesford in Kent there is a restored 13th century friary, a place of peace with a beautiful rose garden. Here is a lovely prayer used by those in retreat there and perhaps one that some of us may like to use:

May every day begin with space
Enough to see my Saviour's face.

May every hour possess within it
The space to live a prayerful minute.

And may I find, from night's alarms,
The space between my Saviour's arms.

SATURDAY—MAY 4.

THE Lady of the House has an excellent antidote for the days when things have tended to get on top of her. She puts on her comfortable shoes and takes a brisk walk to where a bridge crosses a stream. There she picks up a handful of twigs and throws them one by one into the water saying, "That was for the washing that blew off the line, that's for the saucepan I burned, that's for the cross words I spoke — and *that's* because I feel so out of sorts!"

And as the twigs float away, so the things that have irritated her do, too. It's simple, but she says it works, and who am I to argue?

SUNDAY—MAY 5.

HE hath shewed thee, O man, what is good; and what doth the Lord require of thee, but to do justly, and to love mercy, and to walk humbly with thy God? Micah 6:8.

MONDAY—MAY 6.

WE often hear the phrase "Black Monday" but, as this poem "So Cheerful" by Shirley E. Peckham shows, there's no reason at all why we shouldn't enjoy each day of the week!

I smile on Sundays,
It's a day I like;
I smile on Mondays,
As I ride my bike;
I smile on Tuesdays,
As I iron my clothes;
I smile on Wednesdays,
As the wind blows;
I smile on Thursdays,
As I shop in town;
I smile on Fridays
— Why wear a frown?
When it rains on Saturdays,
I smile then, too;
If you were as happy,
So would you!

TUESDAY—MAY 7.

OUR friend, James Carr, is a lay preacher and a lover of Nature. His latter interest seems to coincide naturally with the first. One of his recent sermons was on trees, and I asked him to allow me to quote these words from it:

"The mountain cedar is born to wind and sleet, and lives a long, long time thanks to its tough core and deep roots. The stately palm is nurtured in warm sun and tropic breezes. Its pith is soft and its roots are shallow. It can't survive the hurricane."

It's true of us, too. If our faith is deep and strong enough, we can survive the storms of life.

WEDNESDAY—MAY 8.

HAVE you ever thought of counting your blessings? Literally, I mean.

Freda, a housebound friend of ours, does just that. She's such a contented person and it's always a pleasure to be in her company.

I remember once saying to her, "God bless you" to which she instantly replied, "He does!"

Here is part of Freda's blessings list for just one day:

A long letter from her granddaughter at college.

A visit from a neighbour.

A coloured drawing handed in to her by a four-year-old child.

A phone call from a friend.

A small pot plant left on her doorstep.

A cheeky sparrow hopping on her window sill.

The sight of the first pink cherry blossom.

THURSDAY—MAY 9.

HERE'S a nice story for Ascension Day. After Jesus had ascended into heaven, he was asked what would happen to his Kingdom now that he was no longer on earth.

"I have left behind me eleven men," he said. "I spent three years with them, they know my teaching and my ways and they will carry on my work."

"And what if they fail?" persisted the questioner.

"They must not fail," replied Jesus. "I have no others."

So, because those first disciples were faithful to their task and spread the good news to others, who in their turn did the same, Christianity grew and 2,000 years later it has reached every corner of the earth. It's a thought to inspire us as we celebrate Ascension Day.

FRIDAY—MAY 10.

EVERYBODY likes a person who is contented with his lot. Here is an anonymous verse that expresses the sentiment well:

With a porch at my door, both for shelter and shade,
As the sunshine or rain may prevail,
And a small spot of ground for the use of my spade,
With a barn for the use of my flail;
A cow for my dairy, a dog for my game,
And a purse when a friend wants to borrow,
I'll envy no nabob his riches or fame
Nor what honours await him tomorrow.

SATURDAY—MAY 11.

ONE leg of our old and much-loved kitchen stool needed repair. We couldn't use it when it had only three good legs. However, it didn't take too much mending and soon the stool was standing foursquare on all its legs again.

It struck me that the four legs on the stool are very much like the cornerstones of a person's health — physical, mental, social and spiritual well-being. If one of these four undergoes a temporary setback, then the whole personality is affected and we are thrown off balance. That's when we need the support of others — family and friends — to restore our equilibrium.

SUNDAY—MAY 12.

THE Lord bless thee, and keep thee: The Lord make his face shine upon thee, and be gracious unto thee: The Lord lift up his countenance upon thee, and give thee peace. Numbers 6: 24-26.

LOOKING FORWARD

When the sun's high up in the heavens
And new life stirs the trees —
It's oh, for boots and rucksack,
And a day of "go-as-you-please".

It's then you can face the future
With a bright and ready smile,
And show the world you're willing
To travel that extra mile.

MONDAY—MAY 13.

EVERY year in May, 500,000 volunteers set out to make door-to-door collections for Christian Aid. The money helps towards better health care, education, irrigation and agricultural equipment for the poor of the Third World, so that they may have more resources to help themselves.

I am reminded of Alison Uttley who wrote those delightful children's books in "The Little Grey Rabbit" series. In "The Country Child", she tells how Susan Garland, on her way home from school, turned back guiltily and walked two miles just to pick up a crust she had carelessly dropped.

As this year's appeal is made for the hungry, it would be fitting to remember the tale of Susan Garland and a previous year's Christian Aid slogan: "To live more simply, that others might simply live".

TUESDAY—MAY 14.

A GROUP of would-be young reformers were once holding an informal debate, and agreed that the world was just about as corrupt and bad as it could be.

Then a man standing nearby remarked, "What you seem to want, friends, is a place where everyone has to be good by law."

"That's it!" chorused the reformers enthusiastically.

"A place where no one need worry about food and clothes."

"Yes!" came the reply.

"A place where everyone keeps regular hours."

"That's just what we do want!"

"Well, I've just come from such a place," announced the speaker.

"You have? Where is it?" clamoured several voices.

"It's called prison!" came the reply.

WEDNESDAY—MAY 15.

IN this poem, Margaret H. Dixon reminds us just how grateful we should be for the use of our hands:

I use my hands to wash the floor,
To open wide the kitchen door,
To carry baskets through the street,
To shake the hands of those I meet,
To write a letter to a friend,
To stamp the envelope I send.

I use my hands to drive the car,
On journeys near or journeys far,
To hold a welcome cup of tea,
To wave to friends who smile at me,
To bake the bread, to knead the dough,
To thread a needle, and to sew.

I use my hands to dust the shelf,
To run a bath, to wash myself,
To wipe the tears of little boys,
To mend with care their broken toys,
To blow a kiss to someone dear,
And bring God's Heaven a bit more near.

THURSDAY—MAY 16.

I WAS looking through my desk recently when I came across the autograph album given to me as a present when I was a boy. Amongst the signatures and the humorous verses and sketches that friends and relatives had inscribed, I found this written by one of my teachers:

"One of the greatest lessons of life is to learn not to do what one likes, but to like what one has to do."

FRIDAY—MAY 17.

IT was early Sunday morning. The sun was shining and I thought I was the only person in the park. Then I saw an elderly lady picking up things from the grass. She was collecting discarded bottles and cans in a cardboard box.

She saw me looking and smiled. "I come here every Sunday," she explained. "A lot of people have picnics on Saturday and some — well, they're not very tidy, are they?"

I agreed, but asked, "Don't you feel angry that you should be having to clean up after them?"

"Sometimes I do," she said. "But that never lasts long, and mostly I just wish that another ten people would come and join me."

So, after that, what could I do but lend a hand and help to fill her box!

SATURDAY—MAY 18.

I CAME across a definition the other day which is new to me: "A bore is a person who talks about his rheumatism when you want to talk about yours!"

I think a lot of us need now and again that shrewd little reminder that one of the secrets of happiness is to be more outward-looking, and to overcome our own aches and pains by paying attention to someone else's. Remember the words of the Bible: "The Lord turned the captivity of Job when he prayed for his friends."

SUNDAY—MAY 19.

FOR God, who commanded the light to shine out of darkness, hath shined in our hearts, to give the light of the knowledge of the glory of God in the face of Jesus Christ. Corinthians II 4:6.

MONDAY—MAY 20.

JOHN M. ROBERTSON of Edinburgh sent me these thoughtful lines:

Though Life can oft present us
With problems day by day,
Here's something to remember
Each step along the way —
When you start to count your blessings,
You surely must concede
The sum of all your worries
Is very small indeed.

TUESDAY—MAY 21.

IT was a moment of decision for John McKay. The man who had started his working life as a shepherd lad and had worked long hours over the years to build up successful businesses, now at last had the ticket that would make a dream come true — a flight on Concorde.

Then he decided he wouldn't go. He couldn't bring himself to use it. Instead he raffled the ticket for £3500 for the benefit of Cancer Research.

John McKay and his wife Jean don't only give money to the cause dear to their hearts. They give untold amounts of time. The shepherds' crooks which John has made in his Dumfriesshire home have been purchased by customers all over the world.

I don't suppose anyone knows of all the work the McKays have done for Cancer Research. Just let me say that I have been told that in six years they raised over £25,000.

It's nice to know that, after all, John got his flight on Concorde. His family secretly clubbed together to buy the ticket. He could hardly refuse to use that one, could he?

WEDNESDAY—MAY 22.

A MAN who survived years of captivity in a prisoner-of-war camp in the Last War said afterwards that what kept him going was the knowledge that his family and friends were remembering him daily in their prayers.

The poet Angela Griffiths might have written these lines for him:

Somewhere there's someone who's thinking of you,
Somewhere there's someone who cares.
Your name has been spoken
So hold on in faith,
There's always an answer to prayers.

THURSDAY—MAY 23.

EARLIER this year, I called in to see our friends Fred and Mary. It's only three years since they moved into their new home, but in that time they have transformed an area of rubble and weeds into a glorious garden.

From the start, these devoted partners have worked hard to create a place of beauty. It's quite an achievement, for Fred is 73 and Mary, 71.

I thought the garden had a very special atmosphere and I told Fred so.

He looked thoughtful as he puffed on his pipe. "Not surprising, really, is it?" He smiled. "This garden didn't just happen overnight. It's something Mary and I thought about and planned with care. Now, with love and team-work, our dream has come true."

Love and team-work . . . they're the secret of a happy marriage, a contented family and a lot of other things as well, aren't they?

FRIDAY—MAY 24.

DAVID HUME, the Scottish philosopher, was one of this country's greatest thinkers, but he had a very down-to-earth way of looking at life.

He tells us in his autobiography, written 200 years ago, that to maintain his independence so that he could concentrate on his writing, he was determined to live very simply and economically. He goes on to say:

"I was ever more disposed to see the favourable than the unfavourable side of things, a turn of mind which is more happy to possess than to be born to an estate of £10,000 a year."

I think you'll agree that's every bit as true today.

SATURDAY—MAY 25.

THEY were lovely, all the mothers
Of the days of long ago,
With their gentle, quiet faces
And their hair as white as snow.

They were middle-aged at forty,
At fifty donned lace caps,
And at sixty clung to shoulder shawls
And loved their little naps.

But I love the modern mother
Who can share in all our joys,
And who understands the problems
Of her growing girls and boys.

She may boast that she is older,
But her heart is twenty-three . .
My glorious bright-eyed mother
Who is keeping young with me!

SUNDAY—MAY 26.

WE may sometimes forget the time-honoured custom of saying grace, but that lovable writer G. K. Chesterton never did. In fact, he made a great point of it as he once explained to a friend:

"You say grace before meals. All right. But I say grace before the play and opera, and grace before the concert and pantomime, and grace before I open a book, and grace before sketching, painting, swimming, fencing, boxing, walking, playing, dancing, and grace before I dip the pen in the ink."

A nice reminder of the many good things we should be thankful for.

MONDAY—MAY 27.

DID you know that sweet violets used to be one of the most popular tokens of friendship? In flower language they symbolise innocence and modesty, so they were a fitting gift for a gentleman to buy for a loved one. Oil of violets was a favourite perfume and cards would often bear a picture of a bunch of violets with inscriptions such as "Thinking of you", or "A bunch of violets — what sweeter token, a link in friendship's chain unbroken."

There were violet nurseries in ancient Greece, but one of the most touching stories about them concerns their association with Napoleon and Josephine. On their first meeting, she threw a posy of violets at the young officer's feet. Napoleon kept it and after their marriage, whatever the pressures of battle, he sent her a bunch of violets on every wedding anniversary.

When he was about to be exiled, he asked to visit Josephine's grave. There he picked some violets, and after he died the faded flowers were found in a locket round his neck.

SAFE HAVEN

When the wanderlust has faded
And the anchor dropped at last,
Then it's into friendly waters
Far removed from stormy past.

For no matter where we travel,
Overland, by air or sea,
It's the old, familiar harbours
That are best for you and me.

TUESDAY—MAY 28.

JOYCE FRANCES CARPENTER here expresses the feelings of a young woman in those precious, never-to-be-forgotten early days of marriage:

Each morning as the clock strikes eight,
He sweeps aside his breakfast plate.
Then from the gate I wave goodbye,
Turn back into the house and sigh.
Just look at all those dirty crocks!
And what about his filthy socks?
The sheets to iron, the beds to make,
The floors to clean, the cakes to bake.
I wonder as I grouse all day,
If other young brides feel this way?
Then evening comes. He's at the door,
I rush across the kitchen floor.
He takes me in his strong embrace,
I feel his lips upon my face.
All day I've waited just for this,
His coming home . . . his tender kiss.
The lonely hours of this long day,
Now that he's back, melt right away!

WEDNESDAY—MAY 29.

I SUPPOSE there are times when all of us have to fight against the feeling that we are right and everyone else is wrong.

I remember a sermon in which the minister illustrated this in an amusing way. He said, "There are people who seem to think that the verb 'to be firm' goes, 'I am firm — thou art obstinate — he is pig-headed!'"

If we are honest, I imagine most of us are guilty of this sometimes!

THURSDAY—MAY 30.

SOMETIMES the greatest obstacle we have to overcome in life is our own reluctance to make a start. I found this verse in my old autograph album:

Better to strive and climb and never reach the goal,
Than to drift along with Time, an aimless, worthless soul.
Aye, better to climb and fall, or to sow, and the yield be small,
Than to throw away day after day, and never to strive at all.

Anne Frank, the 14-year-old Jewish girl in Amsterdam, wrote these challenging words shortly before she was dragged off by the Nazis to meet death in the concentration camp: "How wonderful it is that nobody need wait a single moment before beginning to improve the world!"

Someone else once said, "The door of opportunity is marked PUSH."

Let's resolve to make the most of our own opportunities — today.

FRIDAY—MAY 31.

DOES God keep a diary? Mrs White is convinced of it — because one day her minister felt compelled to pay her a call when he was out visiting.

"How did you remember to come today?" she asked, as she ushered him in.

The minister looked surprised until Mrs White reminded him that it was a year ago to the very day that he had conducted her late husband's funeral.

She had been dreading the anniversary, but now the minister had turned up to lighten her load.

A lucky chance? Not in Mrs White's view.

JUNE

SATURDAY—JUNE 1.

THE monks of a certain abbey worked hard tilling their marshy ground. They drained and tended it until the land became fertile and yielded good crops. Their labours of love became widely known and no one was turned away hungry from their doors. They were well regarded by all, yet they had one great sorrow: not one of them had a really good singing voice, and they felt they could not render to God what they considered worthy worship in their chapel.

One day, a stranger, a famous singer with a glorious voice, came to spend the night. He offered to sing with them at their service. At once the monks told him they would remain silent, for they were not fit to mingle their voices with his. And so, at Evensong, he sang the "Magnificat" while they listened and admired.

That night, the Abbot had a dream. An angel from God said to him, "Why was there no praise in the chapel tonight? For years I have listened to it with great joy, but tonight you and your brothers were silent."

Then the Abbot knew that what made sweet music and worthy praise in God's ears was not a finely trained musical voice, but hearts of true love.

SUNDAY—JUNE 2.

THEREFORE we are buried with him by baptism into death: that like as Christ was raised up from the dead by the glory of the Father, even so we also should walk in newness of life. Romans 6:4.

MONDAY—JUNE 3.

STANDING by a narrow country bridge, I looked across at a superb display of bluebells. I was joined by a couple who were being led along the path by guide dogs.

"Good morning," I said. "Aren't the bluebells lovely?"

As soon as I had spoken, I realised my foolish mistake. However, the couple smiled and agreed with me. "Even if we can't see them, we can smell them," the woman laughed.

We chatted for a while and later, as I drove home, I thought of all the brave people who overcome their handicaps with courage and a cheerful spirit. They inspire us all.

TUESDAY—JUNE 4.

OUR next-door neighbours were surprised to find a strange car in their drive when they came home from work one evening. Their first reaction of panic at being unprepared for an unexpected guest soon turned to speculation when they realised it was a brand new car without occupants or possessions inside.

Could this be, at long last, the car they had been trying to win in competitions? The mystery was solved when they went inside the house and found on the mat the car's delivery note meant for a neighbour.

Life is full of surprises, some pleasant, some not so pleasant and some quite shattering, but it's the way we face these ups and downs that matters — whether we allow ourselves to stay down in the dumps or whether we make the best of the situation, pick ourselves up and start all over again. If we remember that there is always hope, no matter how dark things seem, we can face the future with courage.

WEDNESDAY—JUNE 5.

YOUNG Stevie had been paying close attention to his Sunday School teacher and he told me all about it.

"She gave us a kind of numbers game, so that we'd remember special words." He held up his hands and recited proudly: "The seven most important words are — 'I made a mistake, and I'm sorry'. Six — 'You have done a good job'." Stevie kept one hand raised. "The five are — 'And what is your opinion'?" A slight frown creased his brow, then he went on, "Oh, yes, four — 'Can I help you?' and three — 'I appreciate you'."

"Two," he continued. "Well, they're 'Thank you'."

"And the last word?" I prompted.

Stevie replied smartly, "I." And he added, "But we've to remember that's the least important word of all."

THURSDAY—JUNE 6.

OUR old friend Mary lives near enough a small park to be able to take a stroll there, and indeed, she spends many a happy afternoon amongst the flowers. Often she meets somebody she can share a seat with to enjoy a pleasant chat in the sunshine.

In the Spring she told us about a magnificent display of tulips and when the Lady of the House next went to see her, Mary asked if we, too, had admired them. The Lady of the House had to confess, rather shame-facedly, that she hadn't found time to go to the park recently.

"You missed a treat," said Mary quietly.

How often it can happen — a fleeting rainbow, a glorious sunset, a magical frosted spider's web, a raindrop in a flower . . . They pass by all too quickly, and we can miss so many of Nature's wonders if we don't make time to "stand and stare".

FRIDAY—JUNE 7.

THIS verse was discovered in an old autograph album and I thought it well worth passing on:

If you have shared another's load
Or eased another's pain,
If you have soothed a troubled soul
Life has not been in vain.
If you have cheered another's heart
Or made a sad face smile,
If you have calmed another's fear
Your life has been worthwhile.
If you have said a tender word
Or dried another's tears,
If you have spread your share of love
Then you've been needed here.
If you have lent a helping hand
Through times of care and strife,
If you have done a little good
You've made the most of life.

SATURDAY—JUNE 8.

YOUNG Billy who lives next door loves to catch me out with his riddles.

"Mr Gay," he called out over the garden fence, "why do you think my dog would make a good ironmonger?"

"I've no idea," I replied.

"Well, he's just made a bolt for the door," said Billy, chuckling as he ran away.

SUNDAY—JUNE 9.

AND as we have borne the image of the earthly, we shall also bear the image of the heavenly.

Corinthians I 15:49.

MONDAY—JUNE 10.

THERE'S a twittering in the hedgerows,
A chirpy, drowsy stirring;
The little birds are tuning up
As dawn comes creeping slow;
When the sun gilds the horizon
Their chorus will go soaring,
Pouring thanks to their Creator
For another day to go!

Let me open wide my window and listen
To the anthem
As their singing reawakens
My faith in God above.
Let me face this day with courage,
And trust in Him who made us,
And go my way rejoicing in the
Sureness of His love.

Sydney Bell.

TUESDAY—JUNE 11.

JUNE 11th is St Barnabas' Day and the motto for it is "Barnaby bright, all day and no night".

The Bible tells us the name means "Son of Encouragement" for it was Barnabas who helped St Paul and the early Christians by encouraging them to hold fast and by giving practical help and money.

I am reminded of a story about a church that had two stewards, one cheerful and optimistic, the other always a pessimist. Each Sunday the minister was greeted by the first man who said, "Good morning, Minister, there's a nice crowd here and the church is half full already," while the second always said, "Oh, dear, it's half empty as usual."

I know which one I'd like to have known!

MASTER CRAFTSMAN

It's hard to find a better match
Than mellow stone and golden thatch,
And surely he deserves to thrive
Who keeps a dying craft alive,

Whose practised hand reveals his art
Of England's heritage a part.
In preservation he succeeds
And adds his signature in reeds.

WEDNESDAY—JUNE 12.

I AM an amateur beachcomber. Whenever I visit the seashore, I can't resist walking along the tideline to see what the waves have left behind. Sometimes I find things which make me stop and think — and that is what happened recently when I came upon two very different pieces of driftwood. One was beautiful, bleached white by the sun and when I touched it, it felt as smooth as velvet. But the other — the bark was peeling off and I ended up with a splinter in my finger!

The smooth driftwood had been caught up in the ebb and flow of the tide, then beaten against the shore until the edges were smoothed. It had taken on a new beauty. The other piece had a lot more buffeting to endure before it, too, would be smooth.

I couldn't help thinking how like these pieces of driftwood we all are as we endure the storms and knocks of life — and learn to rise above them.

THURSDAY—JUNE 13.

THESE lines were written by Mabel Hall more than 80 years ago:

They talk about a woman's sphere
As though it had a limit,
There's not a place in earth or heaven,
There's not a task to mankind given,
There's not a blessing or a woe
There's not a whispered "yes" or "no",
There's not a life or birth that has
A feather's weight of worth
Without a woman in it!

As a mere man, I grudgingly admit there may be a grain of truth in that!

FRIDAY—JUNE 14.

I HEARD recently of someone who read through the New Testament armed with a red and a black pen. With the black pen, he underlined all the passages to do with sorrow, weeping, pain and death. With the red one, he marked the words dealing with joy, singing, laughter, feasting and the like.

He said that when he then flipped over the pages of his New Testament it seemed to be dominated by red underlining. Where did this idea come from that religion is a gloomy business? The Bible is happy news for us all.

SATURDAY—JUNE 15.

WHEN Peggy became a widow, one of her main problems was loneliness. For a while she had plenty of visitors, but as the months went by they called less frequently, and she felt very much alone.

Then one day a friend suggested that Peggy might volunteer to help at the local sports and social club for handicapped people. Although she is disabled herself, Peggy agreed to give it a try.

Now, two years later, she is the hard-working secretary of the club, and when I last saw her she was surrounded by scores of grateful members. She was certainly looking anything but lonely!

When I think of Peggy, I am reminded of something Dale Carnegie said: "You make more friends by becoming interested in other people than by trying to interest other people in yourself."

SUNDAY—JUNE 16.

VERILY, verily, I say unto you, he that believeth in me hath everlasting life. John 6:47.

MONDAY—JUNE 17.

"IT'S been a grand day, Mr Gay!" called out a cheery neighbour as I strolled down the road. A little farther on, another neighbour gloomily predicted that we were bound to have heavy rain before nightfall and that it would damage the ripening crops.

The world seems to be made up of such optimists and pessimists. There are those who are ready to see the best in things and others who can only see the worst; those who see a promising start has been made on a project and those who think it doomed to failure.

But whatever our own feelings may be, it's an indisputable fact that both sunshine and rain are necessary in life, and it's worth remembering, too, how they often combine to produce the breathtaking beauty of a rainbow.

TUESDAY—JUNE 18.

THE poet Elsie S. Campbell wrote these appealing verses which bear the title "Mirrors":

The tall one in my bedroom
Brightens every day,
But my kitchen mirror
Fills me with dismay!

Small ones in dark corners
Flatter me, I find,
But my handbag mirror
Can be most unkind!

After much reflection
I now realise
The mirrors I look best in
Are my loved one's eyes.

WEDNESDAY—JUNE 19.

DR WILLIAM BARCLAY wrote prayers for many different occasions and here is one for a wedding anniversary:

"O God, I thank you that you have given us another year of life together. I thank you for the love which grows more precious and for the bonds which grow more close each day. I thank you for the happiness we have known together; for the sorrows we have faced together; for the experience of sunshine and shadow through which we have come to today. I ask your forgiveness for any disloyalty on my part; for any times when I was difficult to live with; for any selfishness and inconsiderateness; for any lack of sympathy and of understanding which spoiled even for a moment the perfect relationship which marriage should be.

"Spare us to each other to go on walking the way of life together, and grant that for us it may be true that the best is yet to be."

THURSDAY—JUNE 20.

YOU'VE heard the expression, "pouring oil on troubled waters"? It is attributed to St Aidan who in 635 A.D. founded a monastery on the tranquil island of Lindisfarne or Holy Island, off the coast of Northumbria. The story goes that a young priest was sent to escort King Oswy's bride across the sea and Aidan gave him a cruse of oil to pour on the waves if they got rough. It did become stormy so the priest poured oil on the water, thereby proving the scientific fact that oil reduces wave activity.

There's a good lesson for life here. We can very often restore calm in the disagreement by using a little of the oil of tact and diplomacy.

FRIDAY—JUNE 21.

FOUR-YEAR-OLD Jamie called on me one morning. In his right hand he was clutching a small model car which he held up for my inspection, and proudly said, "My baby sister gave me this."

Well, there's nothing unusual in that, you may say, but it so happens that his baby sister is only a fortnight old! However, I met his father a day or two later, and all was explained.

Apparently, the family was worried that Jamie might feel some jealousy at the baby's arrival after enjoying all the parental attention for four years, so when his father told him to fetch his mother and the new arrival from hospital, Mum was well prepared. Out of the folds of the baby's shawl, she took a tiny model car, saying, "Here is your new sister, Jamie, and she's brought a present for you."

What a wise mother!

SATURDAY—JUNE 22.

SITTING still and wishing
Don't make the country great;
The Lord provides the fishing,
But you've got to dig the bait!

That verse made me smile when I first read it, but the more I thought about it, the more true it seemed. There's no use sitting waiting for the good things to come along — we've got to put in the groundwork first.

SUNDAY—JUNE 23.

WHOSOEVER therefore shall humble himself as this little child, the same is greatest in the kingdom of heaven. Matthew 18:4.

MONDAY—JUNE 24.

YEARS ago I heard a preacher say, "The stars are stupendous, but the little man looking through the telescope is even more wonderful." I have forgotten who the preacher was and I can't remember much about the rest of the sermon, but I think those words will remain with me for ever.

Size isn't everything. In this vast universe we may feel small and insignificant, but we can think, we can worship, we can love, we can help others. These things make us "big" in the true sense of the word. May that thought encourage us today.

TUESDAY—JUNE 25.

THE Lady of the House and I called to see one of our old neighbours who had had to move into a small house without a garden because of poor health. We knew she would miss her lawns and flower borders but were surprised at the way she had already transformed her drab little back yard. She had filled tubs and containers with scarlet geraniums, colourful begonias and marigolds and her hanging baskets were a cascade of fuchsias and trailing lobelia.

"I've chosen the brightest colours I could find," she said, "and what's more I have grown them all myself. In the Autumn I sat at my kitchen table and took cuttings and in the Spring I grew seeds on my sunny window sill — and now that the nice weather has arrived, all I have to do is go round with the watering can and sit in the sun enjoying the blooms."

As we walked home again the Lady of the House remarked, "What a lovely spirit Mrs Slater has! Whatever place becomes her home, she soon makes it into a bright and cheerful spot."

God bless all homemakers.

CRUISING BY

WEDNESDAY—JUNE 26.

ON 26th June, 1913, street collections in aid of Queen Alexandra Rose Day took place for the first time.

The inspiration came from a priest Queen Alexandra had met in her native country, Denmark. He had opened his home to handicapped children and orphans, never turning away anyone in need of help and comfort. Soon it became difficult to find enough money to care for them all. Then he remembered his garden full of beautiful roses — he cut them and sold them to help with the expense of looking after "his" children.

When Alexandra married King Edward VII she devoted much of her time to charitable causes and, remembering the priest, she decided she, too, would sell roses to help those in need. Each year in June, small pink artificial roses are sold throughout Britain and the millions of pounds raised have been shared amongst many charities — needy children, old people, the deaf, the blind; in fact, wherever there is a need to be met.

THURSDAY—JUNE 27.

I WAS sorting through a box of old books at a Girl Guides' jumble sale, when I came across a little leather-bound volume. In it were these words by the American poet and philosopher, Ralph Waldo Emerson:

"God evidently does not intend us all to be rich or powerful or great, but he does intend us all to be friends."

I bought the book to give to a friend, and went home feeling as happy as if I'd found a precious jewel. Isn't it amazing the treasures that can be unearthed in the most unexpected places?

FRIDAY—JUNE 28.

WE had our Sunday School Prizegiving last Sunday and it was heartening to see so many children enjoying singing the hymns, and going forward proudly to receive the prizes they had gained for regular attendance during the year.

I was reminded of Lord Mackintosh, perhaps best known for his toffees, but also as the pioneer of National Savings, an enthusiast for charitable works who had a lifelong association with the Methodist Church. He received many honours, but one he valued highly was a plaque on the wall of the Sunday School he had attended as a boy:

"There was once a boy who was a scholar in this School and later a teacher who became President of the World's Sunday School Association."

Like many other great men, he had received a good foundation in childhood and it had remained throughout his life as his rock and his mainstay.

SATURDAY—JUNE 29.

ISN'T it sad when people say, "I'm feeling blue today", meaning that they are feeling down in the dumps? Blue is such a beautiful colour, and when you count the number of lovely things that are blue — a Summer sky, the sparkling sea, a carpet of bluebells, forget-me-nots, a child's trusting eyes — then surely it's a colour that should make us glad? It does me, and I hope it does the same for you.

SUNDAY—JUNE 30.

AND Jesus looking upon them saith, With men it is impossible, but not with God: for with God all things are possible.

Mark 10:27.

JULY

MONDAY—JULY 1.

I ATTENDED a garden party the other day. I was the only guest, but even so it was a most enjoyable occasion. Tea on the lawn with buttered scones and fresh strawberries must surely be a taste of heaven!

My host was Miss Vincent, a lady who has been involved with gardens all her life. As we sipped tea, she told me, "I look upon flowers as my friends. In this hectic world, flowers have the power to soothe, if we take time to let them."

As I walked home after my visit, I thought about the beautiful flowers that bless Miss Vincent's garden with tranquillity each changing season. Roses, lavender, lily of the valley . . . honeysuckle, heather, sweet peas . . . marigolds, pansies, pinks . . . candytuft, larkspur, lobelia . . .

Yes, even the very names have a soothing effect, don't they?

TUESDAY—JULY 2.

I LIKE this verse by Bridget Charters. It's titled "As I Grow Old", and it reminds us that a sense of humour is a priceless gift — especially when we are able to laugh at ourselves:

Four graces, Lord, I pray
As passing years
Begin to slow me down:
Love, energy,
And fortitude,
These three—
And lastly, laughter
For when the others fail.

WEDNESDAY—JULY 3.

OLDER readers will remember a very popular radio programme of some years ago, "The Brains Trust", in which well-known personalities answered questions on a wide variety of topics put to them by members of the audience.

One popular, if controversial, member of the team on many occasions was Professor C. E. M. Joad, remembered by many of us, in particular, for the way he had of prefixing his answers to questions with the words, "Well, it all depends what you mean by . . ."

On one occasion, the team were discussing the difference between pleasure and happiness and they cited such diverse activities as pottering in the garden on a Summer afternoon, going to the theatre or climbing a mountain, indicating the very different ways in which people find satisfaction.

I remember how Joad dismissed the idea that mere pleasure is the same thing as happiness. He said, "The attempt to secure happiness by a succession of pleasures is as unsatisfying as attempting to get light from striking a succession of matches!"

THURSDAY—JULY 4.

I ONCE saw a group of young people walking in pilgrimage to St Albans Abbey in Hertfordshire where they were to join groups of other youngsters who were converging on the Abbey from all over the county. It must have been a wonderful experience to be travelling along different roads and in different ways, but all going in the same direction — just as we should do in life, in fact.

These energetic young people reminded me of a saying I once read: "If God is going your way, he will give you a lift — if he isn't, then you're on the wrong road!"

FRIDAY—JULY 5.

I LIKE the story about two neighbours who were keen gardeners. Both Mr Hughes and Mr Brown had seen their crops of early peas killed by the frost one Spring.

A little later, Mr Brown came to commiserate with his neighbour. "That was very unfortunate for us, wasn't it? I've done nothing but think about it ever since." He paused to look round, and then asked, "What's that you've got there?"

"Ah," said Mr Hughes, "I sowed another batch immediately after my loss, and now it looks as if I'm going to have a fine healthy crop after all."

A practical reaction is much more positive than simply dwelling on what has gone wrong, isn't it?

SATURDAY—JULY 6.

I ADMIRE a man who can laugh at himself, and is not afraid to appear foolish, as most of us do at times. Full marks then to a Mr Blyth who confessed a slip-up in a letter to "The Times" newspaper.

"I'm going to Andover. Should I sit in any particular part of the train?" he had asked the guard at a railway station.

"It doesn't much matter, sir," was the courteous reply.

Indeed it didn't matter, for, as Mr Blyth discovered, the train wasn't going to Andover!

SUNDAY—JULY 7.

AND the Lord shall deliver me from every evil work, and will preserve me unto his heavenly kingdom: to whom be glory for ever and ever. Amen.

Timothy II 4:18.

H

THURSDAY—JULY 11.

WALKING along our road, I heard singing. It was an elderly neighbour, Elsie, in her garden. I recognised the tune, "Here We Go Round The Mulberry Bush" and paused by the fence to listen. To my amazement I heard,

"Must remember to pay the gas bill tomorrow,
Tomorrow, tomorrow, tomorrow,
Must turn off the oven at 12 o'clock,
At 12 o'clock, at 12 o'clock . . ."

I popped my head over the fence and asked her why the new words for an old song?

"Oh, it's my new way of remembering things," she replied.

"But wouldn't it be enough just to *say* them over and over?"

"Oh, no," she laughed. "If I said them I would worry about them. When I sing them, I don't worry about them at all. The singing keeps me happy!"

I think I'll try it!

FRIDAY—JULY 12.

THESE verses were written by D.L.A. Jepson who captained the Surrey cricket team at the turn of the century. They appeared in a boys' magazine at that time, but they are a good motto for any of us today:

Play with a straight bat, Sonny,
Whatever the pitch may be,
Be it fast and true
Or a slab of glue,
Or parched like a last year's pea.

Play with a straight bat, Sonny,
In the game of life and at school,
You may have hard luck,
You may make a duck,
But stick to the golden rule —
PLAY STRAIGHT!

SATURDAY—JULY 13.

WE all need to exercise a little caution at times—for example, taking care on the roads and being cautious in the spending of money. But caution can be a bad thing if it prevents us from responding warmly to others.

The philosopher, Bertrand Russell, once said, "Of all forms of caution, caution in love is perhaps the most fatal to true happiness."

SUNDAY—JULY 14.

AND God is able to make all grace abound toward you; that ye, always having all sufficiency in all things, may abound in every good work.

Corinthians II 9:8.

TUESDAY—JULY 9.

MARY was sitting in her parlour browsing amongst her storehouse of treasures when I called on her the other day.

"Here are some nice lines I copied out a long time ago," she said, "and I'm so pleased I've found them again. It's a list of ten wishes for a friend."

She read them to me:

Enough happiness to keep you sweet;
Enough trials to keep you strong;
Enough sorrow to keep you human;
Enough hope to keep you happy;
Enough failure to keep you humble;
Enough success to keep you eager;
Enough friends to give you comfort;
Enough faith and courage in yourself to banish depression;
Enough wealth to meet your needs;
Enough determination to make each day a better day than yesterday.

What more could you wish anyone?

SEA DREAMS

MONDAY—JULY 15.

ONE of our neighbours is a keen needlewoman and whenever she calls in for a cup of tea and a chat with the Lady of the House, she brings her bag of handicrafts with her. Every church bazaar and charity sale is the recipient of her skills and every new baby in the neighbourhood receives a cuddly toy made from the bits in her scrap bag.

I think the secret of her success is that she never says, "What shall I have to buy to make this article?" but "What can I make out of the things that I already have?"

It's a good motto for life, I believe. There are some people who are afraid to start a new project, because they think they haven't the time, the money or the opportunities that others may have. It seems a good idea to consider what we already possess — and make the most of it.

TUESDAY—JULY 16.

WHAT hath God wrought!" is an expression of gratitude not confined to church folk or the compilers of ecclesiastical histories. It was also the message on the first telegram ever sent — on the 24th May 1844.

The sender was the inventor of the telegraph, Professor S.P.B. Morse, born in 1791. He also gave his name to the famous Morse Code.

When asked why he chose to send the message he did on the first telegram, Professor Morse humbly replied, "God revealed the telegraph to me in answer to prayer, and not because I was superior to other men."

Indeed, what hath God wrought!

WEDNESDAY—JULY 17.

HAND-WOVEN Turkish carpets are famous for their traditional patterns which contain medallions, birds of paradise, the Tree of Life and windows with their beautiful jewel colours.

Each pattern is unique, carried in the head of the weaver and passed down through the generations from mother to daughter. They are made by very young girls, for only their tiny fingers can manage the fine knotting process, and each carpet takes many months to make.

I was interested to learn that the weavers never go to school or college to learn their craft — their mother is the only teacher.

Isn't this true of so many other things? Whether it be the first time we hear about right and wrong, good behaviour, patience, loyalty . . . most of the great lessons of life are learned in a good home.

Thank God for mothers!

THURSDAY—JULY 18.

A YOUNG man was seen walking along a beach, stopping every now and then to toss an object into the sea. As the onlooker drew nearer, he asked the youth what he was doing.

"These starfish have been stranded on the beach by the tide, and I'm throwing them back into the sea so that they won't die."

"But," said the other, "there are hundreds of them, and the beach goes on for miles, so what difference will your effort make?"

"Well," said the young man, as he threw another one into the sea, "it makes all the difference to this one, doesn't it?"

FRIDAY—JULY 19.

FROM a selection of verses sent to me by Phyllis Ellison I chose two which say more in their few lines each than many an epic poem. Here is the first:

You can't buy a friendship,
It's worth more than gold,
And its value increases
As true friends grow old.

The second verse tells you how to make a friend in the first place:

Some smiles are big,
Some smiles are small,
But the smile that says welcome
Is the best smile of all.

SATURDAY—JULY 20.

"I'VE a new riddle for you, Mr Gay," called my young friend Billy over the garden fence.

"What did the mummy elf give to the baby elf to make him grow?"

"I can't guess, Billy," I replied. "You'll have to tell me."

"Elf-raising flour, of course!" chuckled Billy happily.

SUNDAY—JULY 21.

AND Jesus said unto him, Go thy way; thy faith hath made thee whole. And immediately he received his sight, and followed Jesus in the way.

Mark 10:52.

MONDAY—JULY 22.

SOME years ago, the Lady of the House was laid low with a bad dose of flu and the minister came to visit. Though she was feeling miserable, the call helped to cheer her up a bit. As he left, he told us that he would be praying for us at 11 o'clock that night. I was grateful, but asked why his timing was so precise.

He explained that at that time every day, he kept vigil for all the people he knew who were in special need. I have often remembered the hour and its comforting help, and have prayed, too, in the hope my support will strengthen others.

TUESDAY—JULY 23.

LIFE'S a Supermarket
With shelves that can contain
Chaos and Confusion,
Worry, Grief, and Pain.

Keep looking for the bargains,
And surely you will find
A measure of real pleasure
On the shelf marked, "Peace of Mind".

Gloom is there a-plenty,
But its value must be curbed.
Let it lie beneath the counter,
And remain there undisturbed.

Long before the final check-out,
The incentive's there to see —
Seek the shelf marked "Happiness".
It's on offer, and it's free!

J. M. Robertson.

WEDNESDAY—JULY 24.

WHAT a good idea, I thought, when I heard about a lady who filled her garden with roses, so that when she drew back the curtains on a Summer's morning, the first thing she saw was the beautiful blooms. She said that beginning the day like this helped to keep her in the right frame of mind throughout the hours to come.

Not all of us are fortunate enough to possess a garden, but there are so many things that can help us to start the day well — gratitude for a roof over our heads and a night spent safely; birdsong on a dull day; the anticipation of a pleasant outing.

St. Paul had this to say: "All that is just and pure, all that is lovable and gracious, whatever is excellent and admirable, fill all your thoughts with these things."

THURSDAY—JULY 25.

HAVE you heard the saying "Strong storms make strong trees"? It's another way of saying that trees that have to face storms put down longer and deeper roots in order to survive. The moral is that trials and tribulations help to form character, and the bigger the hardships we are able to overcome, the stronger we become.

The hymn-writer, Love Maria Willis, put it this way:

Father, hear the prayer we offer
Not for ease that prayer shall be,
But for strength, that we may ever
Live our lives courageously.

St Paul expressed the same sentiments when, at the end of a life of severe testing, he wrote: "I have fought a good fight, I have finished my course, I have kept the faith."

FRIDAY—JULY 26.

FEELING a little down today? Then here are some words of Arnold Bennett's to remind you — and me — how fortunate we are:

"You wake up in the morning and lo! your purse is magically filled with 24 hours of the universe of your life. It is yours. It is the most precious of possessions. No one can take it from you. It is unstealable and no one receives either more or less than you receive."

Now, don't you feel glad to be alive?

SATURDAY—JULY 27.

DOROTHY M. LOUGHRAN sent me a copy of her little book of poems, "Beyond The Hill". I enjoyed all her verses, but this is my favourite:

At the end of the tunnel
There's always a light,
There's always the dawning
After the night,
Always the solace
After the pain,
Ever the sunshine
After the rain;
Look up at the rainbow
Arched in the sky,
A symbol of promise
When things go awry.

SUNDAY—JULY 28.

AND we know that all things work together for good to them that love God, to them who are the called according to his purpose. Romans 8:28.

COUNTRY ROAD

MONDAY—JULY 29.

THERE is an old Jewish story about a widow who visited a Rabbi for advice. She told him she had two sons, one a gardener and the other a potter. The gardener had asked her to pray for rain to water his plants, while the potter had asked her to pray for sunshine to dry his pots.

"What should I do, Rabbi?" she pleaded.

The Rabbi's answer came without a moment's hesitation: "You will do best to leave it in the hands of God."

TUESDAY—JULY 30.

ASK people what their favourite flower is and I expect quite a few will say, "roses". Some, though, would prefer a bloom which didn't also prick your finger!

It can be quite painful, I agree, but when I feel a jab I remind myself of a saying I heard years ago:

"Some people are always grumbling that roses have thorns: I am thankful that thorns have roses".

Try it next time it happens to you.

WEDNESDAY—JULY 31.

I WONDER if you know of this traditional old welcome:

Come in the evening, come in the morning,
Come when expected, or come without warning.
Thousands of welcomes you'll find here before you.
The oftener you come, the more we'll adore you.

How I would enjoy visiting a home with that displayed in the hallway!

AUGUST

THURSDAY—AUGUST 1.

HAVE you heard the story about the little boy who came downstairs one morning to find his mother looking in the cake tin with a puzzled expression on her face?

"There were two pieces of cake when I put it away last night, and now there's only one," she said. "Thomas, can you explain what happened?"

"Yes, Mum," Thomas replied. "It was so dark I couldn't see the other piece!"

FRIDAY—AUGUST 2.

THE late William Lyon Phelps, a distinguished professor of literature at Yale University, once told how on a blazing hot Summer's day he went for lunch in a crowded railway dining car. When the waiter brought him the menu, Phelps remarked, "I feel sorry for the folk working in the kitchen on a day like this."

The attendant looked at him in astonishment and said, "People come in here and complain about the food and the service and grumble at the heat. In all the years I have been doing this job, you are the first person who has given one word of sympathy for the staff in the kitchen where it's even hotter."

It was Phelps's turn to be astonished then. It had never occurred to him that he was doing anything unusual in expressing his appreciation of those "slaving away over a hot stove". Being the kind of person he was, it seemed the most natural thing in the world to think of others. Would that there were more like him!

SATURDAY—AUGUST 3.

HAVE you come across this anonymous old poem before? Its title is " Do It!"

Don't talk about things you are going to do,
Don't say that you mean to be noble and true,
Don't wait till tomorrow to make up your mind
That you'll make others happy, and always be kind;
For tomorrow you'll talk as you're talking today,
And your good resolutions will vanish away.
Do it now—let the world see you mean to be true!
Oh! don't talk of the things you are going to do!

SUNDAY—AUGUST 4.

SALUTE one another with an holy kiss. The churches of Christ salute you. Romans 16:16.

MONDAY—AUGUST 5.

BITTERNESS about something that has happened in the past is one of the most unattractive and destructive of feelings.

Dr. Norman Vincent Peale, noted for his positive approach to life, once asked President Hoover how he prevented himself from becoming embittered during a period of great criticism.

"I'm a Quaker," was the gentle reply.

Dr. Peale knew what he meant, for Quakers believe that if you empty your heart of resentment and bitterness you will receive a God-given inner calm that is not likely to be disturbed by man-made storms.

Another wise man, George Herbert, had this to say: "He who cannot forgive, breaks the bridge over which he himself must pass."

TUESDAY—AUGUST 6.

I WAS amused to find the cat from next door curled up on a shelf in my greenhouse. He had found his way in through a broken pane and was sleeping comfortably out of the cold wind. When he heard me, he just opened an eye, stretched, and went back to sleep.

Cats are well known for their ability to make themselves at home in any situation. Somehow they always manage to find the softest chair or the warmest spot in the house. They can make us feel more comfortable, too. Many people find it relaxing to stroke a purring cat, and because of their therapeutic value, residents in many homes for the elderly are encouraged to keep their cat.

I left my uninvited guest where he was. Maybe later on, I'll get that pane mended, but for the present I'll leave it the way it is. It's my way of thanking the cat tribe for all they do for us, and especially for old folk.

WEDNESDAY—AUGUST 7.

I HAVE been re-reading one of my favourite J.B. Priestley novels, "The Good Companions." It's the story of a group of people who came together in a series of chance encounters and spent a short, happy time as a successful company of roving players. Each had a need, each had something to offer to the others and, in the end, they went their separate ways happier and more fulfilled for having known one another.

That's like life, isn't it? Along the way we meet those who enrich our lives, whose advice we value and whose company we enjoy, who encourage us and share our burdens — and who, in turn, we are able to help.

THURSDAY—AUGUST 8.

ALICE CHRISTIANSON of St Catherine's, Ontario, Canada, sent me this delightful poem:

I like to walk at dawning
When all the world seems new,
As the birds begin their chorus
And the grass is kissed with dew.

I like to walk at midday
When the sun is high above,
And the breeze is flower-scented
With the fragrances I love.

I like to walk at evening,
When all the world is still,
And the feathered folk are homing
To roost beyond the hill.

FRIDAY—AUGUST 9.

SEVEN-YEAR-OLD Roger was spending his summer holiday with his aunt. Nearby lived a blind man, and the boy's sympathy was aroused as he watched him tapping his way around the village with his white stick.

One day Roger said to his aunt, "Auntie, I can't understand it. Mr Smith is still blind, although every night in my prayers, I have asked God to give him his sight back."

Roger's aunt tried to explain that God doesn't always answer our prayers exactly as we ask. The little boy thought for a few moments, and then commented, "Well, in that case, I'll ask God to see that Mr Smith doesn't get run over or hurt."

SATURDAY—AUGUST 10.

A NON-CHURCHGOER was in hospital for an operation, and one morning met the surgeon who was to operate. The surgeon was a practising Christian, and during the conversation said so. The patient replied that he could not see the need for churches, as he could worship God just as well in the open air.

"Quite right," said the surgeon. "And I could operate on you just as well in the middle of the street. Shall I do that?"

SUNDAY—AUGUST 11.

GOD is faithful, by whom ye were called unto the fellowship of his Son Jesus Christ our Lord.

Corinthians I 1:9.

MONDAY—AUGUST 12.

WHEN the Lady of the House and I visited our old friend Mary, she proudly showed us her new budgie in its cage by the window. Its chatter is good company for her and its antics keep her amused for hours. One of its toys is a little plastic man, weighted at the bottom so that however many times the bird knocks it over, it always bounces back.

"That little doll is a real encouragement to me," confided Mary one day. "Whenever I get disappointed or feel 'down', I follow the example of Billy's little man and jump up again. After all, it's no good sitting down and feeling sorry for yourself — you've got to pick yourself up and get on with things."

As I have mentioned before, we always come away from Mary feeling better for her company. This time we felt stronger, too.

TUESDAY—AUGUST 13.

MY jewels are in my garden,
And who can gauge their worth?
I look at them and feel myself
The richest man on Earth.

They're gems of priceless beauty,
Investments very rare.
With such jewels in my garden,
Am I not a millionaire?

J.M. Robertson

WEDNESDAY—AUGUST 14.

THE meter reader called the other morning. He came up the path whistling and smiling broadly. "You're full of the joys of life this morning!" I said.

He told me he had just read the meter at Mrs Andrews' house. Well, I couldn't see why that should have made him so happy, for Mrs Andrews is a rather lonely person who greatly misses her daughter who has just moved away. Apparently, while the meter reader was there, the girl from the florist's had called with a huge bouquet. The intriguing thing was, there was no indication who the sender was.

"What, no message at all?" I exclaimed.

"Oh, yes, there was a message," he said. "On a card was written, 'From a friend who is thinking of you with love', and now Mrs Andrews is going through all the people she knows trying to decide who would do such a wonderful thing. She's so thrilled, she's made me feel happy, too."

"And you've made *me* happy!" I exclaimed, and soon afterwards shared the story with the Lady of the House. And I've no doubt she, in turn, passed on this cheerful story, and so the smile chain goes on . . .

THURSDAY—AUGUST 15.

IN his novel "Rough Justice", C. E. Montague recounts a conversation between two youngsters as they put their toys away at the end of the day.

"Father had a good plan for me today," said Auberon. "He made me have my rest in a sunny place after dinner."

"I think all Father's plans are good," said his sister Molly thoughtfully.

There was a pause while Auberon considered this and then said, "Yes, very."

Molly, too, considered her next remark before saying, "I think he has a big plan in his heart and all the little plans come out of it."

A rather ponderous conversation perhaps for children, yet doesn't it illustrate what many of us feel about God? He had one big plan — the sending of Jesus Christ into the world, and all His other good plans for us spring from that.

FRIDAY—AUGUST 16.

ONE glorious Summer day, the Lady of the House and I were enjoying a picnic, when we noticed a change among the wild flowers around us. Within the space of a few minutes the daisies had closed their petals and the buttercups had dropped their pretty yellow heads. Then the rain started.

Fortunately for us, it was only a brief shower, so the sudden change in weather did not spoil things. In fact, it started me thinking. Those clever little wild flowers had known exactly the right moment to turn their petals into miniature umbrellas! Perhaps our weather-forecasters should keep a plot or window-box and grow wild flowers in it. They might learn a thing or two!

OLD FAVOURITES

When it comes to sharing pleasures
And the sun is overhead,
You'll find that good old-fashioned
Fun and humour aren't dead.

For the younger generation
It's exciting, bright and new,
And in watching their enjoyment
All around will share it, too.

SATURDAY—AUGUST 17.

AMONGST a group of poems sent me by Dorothy M. Loughran, the Winchester writer, I particularly liked this one:

There's always the other side
To the coin,
Life's never so bleak as it seems,
Turn over the page
And you may find
Fulfilment of your dreams.

It's never the same
On the other side,
There's always a different view,
Opportunity's gate
May be opening wide,
And opening —
Just for you.

SUNDAY—AUGUST 18.

AND he said unto them, Go ye into all the world, and preach the gospel to every creature.

Mark 16:15.

MONDAY—AUGUST 19.

I OFTEN spend a few minutes browsing through a dictionary. It's amazing what you notice. Recently, for instance, it occurred to me that there's a group of words that all have something in common. They are words like unassuming, unbiased, unconquerable, undaunted, understanding, unflinching, united, and untiring.

What have they in common? Well, they all start with "U", don't they?

TUESDAY—AUGUST 20.

COLOURS are full of meaning, aren't they?

White is purity, freshly fallen snow, a baby's christening robe, a young girl's first communion dress, a bride's wedding gown.

Black is darkness, but also the night sky studded with stars.

Grey is gloom, aging hair — and doves and dappled horses.

Brown is the earth, a sun tan, tawny owls and nuts.

Red is warmth, fires, ruddy cheeks and blushes, the robin's breast and holly berries.

Green is the life force, grass and trees.

Yellow is sunshine, buttercups and lemons.

Blue is depression, but also the sea, the sky, a forget-me-not, a sapphire.

All these colours weave through our lives to create a rich tapestry of experience. Where would we be without them to help us set our moods?

WEDNESDAY—AUGUST 21.

IN this season of holidays and travel, I thought that this poem "Bargain Break" by Phyllis Ellison has something to say to us all:

She'd obviously had a good time,
So much she had to tell,
Her travels had done her a world of good,
And she related her tales so well.

I said it must have been costly,
She gave me a teasing look,
Oh, no, my dear, it cost me nothing
But the price of a picture book!

MELLOW THOUGHTS

Where willows droop to water
And birdsong fills the air,
Who would not gladly linger
For quiet moments there?

Troubled hearts find solace,
Cares are left behind;
Nature's wondrous beauty
Brings calm and peace of mind.

THURSDAY—AUGUST 22.

WHEN I called in to see my friend Lucy, she was polishing some apples and arranging them in a dish on her sideboard.

"So you even polish the apples!" I teased her, for Lucy is very houseproud.

She held one up. It was rosy red and shining bright. "Don't you think it looks welcoming?" she said. "Like a smiling face!"

I had to admit it — a smile does make all the difference, doesn't it?

FRIDAY—AUGUST 23.

A LONG time ago I had a picnic lunch on the top of Milan Cathedral, which had only recently been officially completed.

It is a fine building, and there is much in it of interest, but what caught my attention were the three portals. The first has a wreath of flowers carved over it, with the inscription: "All that pleases passes away". Over the second is a cross, with the words: "All that troubles passes away". The third and central portal bears the motto: "That only is, which is eternal".

I thought of this when a friend's cousin wrote to tell me that her fiancé had asked her, under a similar portal: "Can't we be more than just friends?" They unconsciously adopted that gateway, or portal, as the symbol of their love, and they now have miniature gateways all over their home. I suppose you might call such sentiment the decor of the heart.

The Milan portals are a parable of life, aren't they? Pleasure doesn't last forever, and trouble doesn't last forever, but as St. Paul reminded his readers, the things that do last for ever are the fruits of the Spirit — especially love.

SATURDAY—AUGUST 24.

I LIKE the legend which describes how a beautiful vision appeared to a monk. In silent bliss he gazed on it — and then noticed it was time for him to take food to the poor of the district. Sadly he turned and left to perform his duties.

When he returned, he was delighted to find the vision still there, waiting for him. As he gazed on it, he heard these words: "If you had stayed, I would have fled."

SUNDAY—AUGUST 25.

KNOW ye not that ye are the temple of God, and that the Spirit of God dwelleth in you?

Corinthians I 3:16.

MONDAY—AUGUST 26.

THE Spring flowers in Jane's garden always seem to be the first to show cheerful colour. In Summer her plot is again a mass of bright blooms, and come the Autumn, her flowers are the last to succumb to the cold of Winter.

One day, as I was admiring her roses, I asked why her garden always seemed so much more colourful than any of the others round about; perhaps she had that mysterious gift of "green fingers"? For a moment she seemed at a loss for an answer, and mentioned the usual gardening tasks — good digging, keeping down weeds . . . then suddenly, she smiled. "But perhaps it's because I always *expect* the best from all my plants," she said.

It's the same with people, isn't it? Distrust them, and they're almost certain to let you down. Look for the best, and they'll give it time after time.

TUESDAY—AUGUST 27.

IN Salt Lake City, the capital of Utah in the USA, stands a granite monument on a pedestal. It is surmounted by a ball on top of which sit two bronze gulls.

This serves as a reminder of a time in the mid-19th century when emigrants to that area had sown 5000 acres of previously barren desert with barley and wheat, and were looking forward to the harvest which would feed the thousands of newcomers to Salt Lake City.

However, in June a great swarm of black crickets attacked the crop, and all attempts to destroy the insects were of no avail. Then they took counsel together and some of the Christians among them recommended a day of prayer. They set apart a day to seek God's help, and prayed all day.

Soon afterwards, a great flock of large white seagulls flew over and began to eat the crickets. They also fed the insects to their young ones, and so the crop was saved.

Coincidence, folk lore or the power of prayer? The local Red Indians had no doubt. They regarded the seagulls as angels from the Home of the Great Spirit, and in gratitude they erected the granite monument to say so.

WEDNESDAY—AUGUST 28.

I HAVE heard and read many recipes for a happy marriage, but I think this little verse by Ogden Nash puts the whole secret in a nutshell:

To keep your marriage brimming
With love in the loving cup,
If ever you're wrong, admit it,
If ever you're right, shut up!

NATURE'S PATTERNS

THURSDAY—AUGUST 29.

A YOUNG actor had joined Scarborough's Theatre-in-the-Round, and before long was complaining to the Director, Stephen Joseph, about the character he had to play. He didn't think the part was well-written.

Joseph told him, "All right, if you can write a better play, I'll put it on in this theatre."

The actor took up the challenge and wrote a play called "The Square Cat". It was a success and its author, Alan Ayckbourn, has gone on to write many more. Today he is one of our most successful playwrights.

He has had ups and downs, of course. There have been failures, and at one point he almost decided to give up. Every new play is a fresh challenge, just like any new venture any of us undertake. Sometimes we forget it takes just as much courage for those at the top of the ladder as it does for the rest of us lower down.

FRIDAY—AUGUST 30.

THE Greek poet Euripides once remarked, "It is a good thing to be rich, and a good thing to be strong — but it is a better thing to be beloved of many friends."

SATURDAY—AUGUST 31.

I LIKE the story I heard about little Catherine whose father's hobby is photography. She's well used to seeing him taking pictures and, needless to say, she's often in them herself.

One day, she and her mother were coming home just as a thunderstorm was starting. At the first flash of lightning Catherine said, "Oh no, Mummy — God has started taking photographs, too!"

SEPTEMBER

SUNDAY—SEPTEMBER 1.

BLESSED be the Lord God of Israel; for he hath visited and redeemed his people. Luke 1:68.

MONDAY—SEPTEMBER 2.

I WAS spending a nostalgic half hour with my old autograph album recently and I came across this entry:

The place where we are treated best and grumble most — HOME.

It was a sobering comment and I was glad to see the other side of the coin put by Myrtle V. Sheppard in her poem about the blessings of a home:

Peace dwells here, and quiet security;
And love stripped bare of selfishness,
Makes homely tasks beneath this roof, true sacraments.

Home, sweet home — there's no place like it!

TUESDAY—SEPTEMBER 3.

WHEN Stanley Baldwin was Prime Minister, he was visited one day at Chequers by a friend who recounted his experiences on a recent trip to the Far East. It was a grim recital of plots, counter-plots, oppression and vice.

At the end of his story, both men sat for some moments in a silence of depression. Then Baldwin pointed to a bowl of roses on the table, and said to his friend, "Bury your face in those roses, and thank God for beauty."

It's advice we can all follow. The beauties of God's creation can always wash us clean.

AUTUMN EASE

WEDNESDAY—SEPTEMBER 4.

HANDS always have a very special significance. In her book "Ten Fingers for God", Dorothy Clarke Wilson tells about Dr. Paul Brand who worked with leprosy patients in India.

Sometimes they would all gather together in fellowship. One evening, Paul joined them, and they asked him to speak. He had nothing prepared yet he willingly stood up, paused for a moment and looked at their hands, some with no fingers, and some with only a few stumps. Then he spoke:

"I am a hand surgeon, so when I meet people I can't help looking at their hands. I would like to have examined Christ's hands. With the nails driven through, they must have appeared twisted and crippled — for remember, Jesus, at the end, was crippled too."

The patients, on hearing this, suddenly lifted their poor hands towards Heaven. Hearing of God's response to suffering had made *their* suffering easier.

Many people will remember Dr. Paul Brand — not just for his healing hands — but for his thoughtful and caring heart.

THURSDAY—SEPTEMBER 5.

TODAY I would like to share with you a poem sent to me by Hazel Aitken of Glasgow.

I simply do not have the time
— I hope she'll understand—
To greet her as she settles in
Or lend a helping hand.
I meant to knock upon her door,
I meant to say "hello",
I meant . . . oh, what's the use of that?
I'll just down tools — and go!

FRIDAY—SEPTEMBER 6.

A CHILD was critically ill in a Devonshire country cottage, and her younger sister Joyce heard the doctor say as he left the house, "Nothing but a miracle can save her."

Joyce went to her money-box, emptied it, and then went to shop after shop in the village street, asking, "Please, I want to buy a miracle." From each shop she came away disappointed. Even the local chemist had to say, "My dear, we don't sell miracles here."

But outside the shop two men had overheard, one of them a doctor from Great Ormond Street Hospital in London. After asking Joyce to explain what she wanted, the doctor went with her to the cottage, examined the patient, and remarked, "It's true — only a miracle can save her, and it must be performed at once."

So saying, he collected his instruments, performed the operation, and the patient's life was saved.

A miracle? I don't know, but it sounds very like it to me.

SATURDAY—SEPTEMBER 7.

IT was the Lady of the House who reminded me of one of the wise sayings of Socrates — "Study to *be* what you wish to *seem*".

We have only to look around us at those who have been successful in sport, music, literature, cooking — or at conquering a quick temper — to realise that success doesn't come cheaply. It is when we are prepared to devote time and effort to our pursuits that we find our true reward. In most things nothing is achieved without perseverance and hard work.

The old saying is still very true: "Don't put your wishbone where your backbone ought to be!"

SUNDAY—SEPTEMBER 8.

MEN and brethren, children of the stock of Abraham, and whosoever among you feareth God, to you is the word of this salvation sent.

Acts 13:26.

MONDAY—SEPTEMBER 9.

WHEN life gets us down and we feel dejected and dispirited, often a ray of hope shines through when least expected. I think this anonymous poem expresses it very well:

Light after darkness,
Gain after loss,
Sweet after bitter,
Crown after cross.
Strength after weakness.
Hope after fears,
Home after wandering,
Joy after tears.

TUESDAY—SEPTEMBER 10.

THERE'S a story about a teacher who held up a sheet of white paper with a tiny black dot in the centre and asked his class what they could see. Every child picked out the black spot — none said they saw the white paper!

It's one of the weaknesses of human nature that we are often more ready to criticise another person than we are to recognise their good points.

It was a 17th century Frenchman, the Duc de la Rochefoucauld who wrote: "If we had no faults we would not take so much pleasure in noticing them in others".

Food for thought, indeed.

TOGETHERNESS

Show the world a happy face,
Have faith in what's in store,
Keep in step with trusted friend
As life holds wide the door.

Stand together, side by side,
Closer grow each day,
Sure of one another's love —
This is harmony.

WEDNESDAY—SEPTEMBER 11.

BADEN POWELL, founder of the Scout Movement, loved kites — they were his hobby and there was not much that he did not know about them. When he was an Army Officer in the Boer War, he experimented with kites, and even tried to lift men into the air with them!

Marconi, the pioneer of wireless, was experimenting with his plans to send the first signals from Cornwall to Canada. He found that in Canada he would need to raise his aerial high in the air, but had no time to erect masts.

He had heard about Baden Powell and his kites but had never met him. In his dilemma, he apprehensively contacted the great man and explained the problem. Of course, Baden Powell graciously let him have suitable kites to take to Canada, where they held up Marconi's aerial wire — in a gale — and enabled the famous signal to be heard.

When I hear this inspiring story I always like to think that the first wireless signal to Canada was thanks to an act of gracious co-operation between two great minds.

THURSDAY—SEPTEMBER 12.

HOW easy it is to speak without thinking and hurt another's feelings, especially when we are living in today's busy, stressful world. Anne Kreer's poem "Hasty Words" gives us all something to think about:

You've said a thoughtless word,
Although you didn't really mean it.
What can you do to take it back,
How best can you redeem it?
Just say "I'm sorry, let's be friends",
That's the best way
To make amends.

FRIDAY—SEPTEMBER 13.

IN the remote Kashmir Valley of India, the authorities understand the value of trees and they do all they can to encourage people to protect them. Along roadsides are signs bearing various messages, of which these are only a few:

WOOD IS GOOD, BUT TREES ARE BETTER.
WE HAD BETTER BE WITHOUT GOLD THAN TREES.
A TREE PLANTED BY A BELIEVER IS A SOURCE OF BLESSING TO HIM AND AN EVERLASTING CHARITY.
THE FOREST AFFORDS PROTECTION TO ALL BEINGS, OFFERING SHADE EVEN TO THE AXEMEN WHO DESTROY IT.

SATURDAY—SEPTEMBER 14.

AS a young man, the Russian writer Dostoevsky was sent to a hard labour camp in Siberia. Throughout his life he was dogged with ill health, domestic worries and financial problems. Yet his spirit never failed and he wrote these inspiring words:

"Love all God's creation, the whole and every grain of sand in it. Love every leaf, every ray of God's light. Love the animals, love the plants, love everything. If you love everything, you will perceive the divine mystery in things. Once you perceive it, you will begin to comprehend it better every day, and you will come at last to love the whole world with an all-embracing love.

"Love the animals: God has given them the rudiments of thought and joy untroubled. Do not trouble it, do not harass them, do not deprive them of their happiness, do not work against God's intent."

SUNDAY—SEPTEMBER 15.

IF any man serve me, let him follow me; and where I am, there shall also my servant be; if any man serve me, him will my Father honour. John 12:26.

MONDAY—SEPTEMBER 16.

THE Lady of the House and I were enjoying one of our favourite pastimes, rummaging round an antique shop, when we came across an old plaque with this verse on it:

Who learns and learns,
Nor acts on what he knows,
Is one who ploughs and ploughs,
But never sows . . .

It was a timely reminder that the way we handle the opportunities given to us is largely up to ourselves. As Dr Norman Vincent Peale wrote: "Never minimise life's possibilities".

TUESDAY—SEPTEMBER 17.

PRUNING roses in Autumn is a sad task. I confess I feel a little guilty as I cut away the beauty of Summer to ensure next year's blooms.

But when I look at the pile of pink, red, white and yellow petals at my feet, the words of an old verse come to mind:

Roses fair on thorns do grow,
And they tell me even so,
Sorrows into virtues grow.

So, although I'm sorry to have to cut away the remains of Summer, I know that, like the virtues, next year's roses will grow anew.

WEDNESDAY—SEPTEMBER 18.

I'M always delighted when I receive an invitation to the Harvest Service at our local primary school. It's one of the highlights of the year to see the lovely array of gifts of produce and the bright little faces as the children sing hymns, recite poems and perform a little play for their parents.

In his talk one year, the minister told us the story about John Chapman who travelled across America in the 1800's planting apple seeds and so became known as "Johnny Appleseed". The point the minister wanted to make to the children was that they should try to sow a seed of goodness each day — a smile, a friendly word or a helpful act, something that would grow into fine trees like the apple seeds in America. And because of what they left behind, the world would be a much better place.

A good thought for us all at any time of year.

THURSDAY—SEPTEMBER 19.

I CAN'T remember exactly
The colour of your eyes,
Or whether your hair was brown or black,
But I know you were always wise.
I can't remember the dress you wore
Though I know that an old friend should
Or whether your nose was long or short,
But I know you were always good.
For the thing that I remember,
That matters in the end,
Is not how you looked at a certain time —
I remember you were my friend.

Jean Harris.

HEAVEN SENT

FRIDAY—SEPTEMBER 20.

HAVE you heard the ten-second sermon, "If you can't make light of your troubles, keep them dark"? It's another way of saying "Laugh and the world laughs with you, weep and you weep alone".

Very few of us manage to go through life without meeting trouble of some sort on the way. It's how we face it that matters; whether we pass on our gloom to everyone we meet, or endeavour to put a brave face on our problems.

The latter course is so worth the effort, both for ourselves and everybody else!

SATURDAY—SEPTEMBER 21.

I HAVE always been fascinated by the little square boxes provided in many shops and public buildings. They have a glass front shielding a button, and the instructions: "In case of fire, break glass".

I didn't know until recently, however, that these emergency boxes owe their origin to one of England's most famous novelists, who admitted to having a great dread of fire.

Charles Dickens suggested knocking a brick or two out of a wall, and covering the hole with glass. "If there's a fire," he said, "the glass can be easily broken in order to get at the keys so that the building might be entered by firemen and rescuers."

This gave the Fire Brigade the idea of providing the alarms we now see everywhere. Charles Dickens's fear led to a device which must have saved countless lives.

SUNDAY—SEPTEMBER 22.

DANIEL answered and said, Blessed be the name of God for ever and ever: for wisdom and might are his.

Daniel 2:20.

MONDAY—SEPTEMBER 23.

"WHAT is love?"

That was the question asked by the young blind and deaf Helen Keller. It was a completely new word to her, and she couldn't understand what it meant — it had no feel to it. And then how wonderfully her inspired teacher, Miss Sullivan, explained the abstract idea to her:

"At the moment you can feel the hot Southern sun, but presently the clouds will cover the sun. You cannot feel the clouds, you know, but you feel the rain and know how glad the flowers and thirsty earth are to have it after the hot day. You cannot touch love, either, but you feel the sweetness that it pours into everything. Without love you would not be happy."

When, in later life, Helen Keller wrote about her first understanding of this beautiful truth, she added: "I felt that there were invisible lines stretched between my spirit and the spirits of others."

TUESDAY—SEPTEMBER 24.

THE other day I was shown a lovely Russian toy shaped like a brightly-coloured turnip. I was told that it depicts a Russian folk tale.

The story tells how a farmer could not move a turnip by himself, so he enlisted the help of his wife but to no avail. Then his daughter joined in, but it still would not move, so the cat was brought from the house. Although they all pulled together, the turnip simply would not budge. Finally, the daughter fetched her pet mouse. When they all pulled hard together, the turnip moved at last.

We do not have to search for the moral of the story — a small contribution can help to achieve great results.

WEDNESDAY—SEPTEMBER 25.

IN these days of exotic holidays you often meet people who seem to have been everywhere. Our own excursions seem modest and small by comparison. It was a comfort to read these words by A. Cooke: "I don't know who said travel broadens the mind, but he could have added that the broader the mind, the thinner it gets. Some of the shallowest people in the world have been everywhere on every continent and seen everything through the eyes of a travel folder."

How very true! It's a timely reminder that there are many good things to be seen much nearer home if we have eyes to see them.

THURSDAY—SEPTEMBER 26.

A FAVOURITE book of my childhood was "Pollyanna", and the "Glad Game" the little girl learned to play is one which has proved its worth for *me* right through life.

Pollyanna's father was an underpaid missionary. They relied greatly on the annual Missionary Box for renewal of clothes and other goods. One year Pollyanna longed passionately for a doll — instead, when they unpacked the box, the only "extra" object was a pair of crutches!

So began the Glad Game: "We must be glad we don't need them," said her father with a rueful smile. From then on, Pollyanna always strove to look for something to be glad about, even when life was grim.

Remember, too, these words written by Lord Byron: "Always laugh when you can: merriment is a philosophy not well understood. It is the sunny side of existence".

FRIDAY—SEPTEMBER 27.

ALONG the path that lies ahead,
What shall I find there?
Shall I find a quiet spot
To meditate in prayer?

A shady bower, a peaceful nook
Tall trees along the way,
A place to read a favourite book
Where Summer breezes play?

Shall I achieve my hopes and dreams
In all that's good and true,
And find — meandering — a stream
That winds to pastures new?

What do we seek along Life's road
What do we hope to find?
Perhaps the greatest gift of all —
Contentment, peace of mind.

Dorothy M. Loughran.

SATURDAY—SEPTEMBER 28.

HERE'S an old harvest-time prayer, which is as relevant this year as ever it was:

Help us to share, for the letters of SHARE are in HARVEST,
Forgive us if we have too much, for the letters of HAVE are in HARVEST,
Help us to save and not to waste, for the letters of SAVE are in HARVEST,
Help those who starve, for the letters of STARVE are in HARVEST.

May we who have too much, learn to share our Harvest with those who have too little.

SUNDAY—SEPTEMBER 29.

CALL unto me, and I will answer thee, and shew thee great and mighty things which thou knowest not. Jeremiah 33:3.

MONDAY—SEPTEMBER 30.

MABEL JEEVES, born in 1892, was a remarkable lady. At the age of 17, when there was little treatment available for tuberculosis, she developed a TB hip. A year or two later, it spread to her spine and from then until her death in 1949 she had to lie flat on her back.

The courage with which she faced her illness was an inspiration to all who knew her, and her sickroom at Newport Pagnall, Buckinghamshire, was a place of love and joy with a steady stream of visitors. She had known family sorrow, but her strong Christian faith upheld her constantly and she published booklets of verse and prose, written under great physical difficulty, which helped people all over the world.

I quote from her writing: "Wonderful, radiant, unfulfilled dreams could come to mind to make one thoroughly sorry for one's particular lot, if they were allowed to come right in to one's heart and mind! But, instead, one thinks of the wonderful, countless gifts received . . . love and friendship; sight; speech and hearing: all these are but a few of the multitude of gifts and blessings which, as we read sometimes in a list of wedding gifts, are, too numerous to mention."

Other inspiring words she wrote were, "If a shut-in invalid can find so much cause for rejoicing in the Lord and in his love-gifts, surely those who can see and enjoy still more of his wonderful universe and his marvellous gifts can find even more cause to rejoice and be thankful."

Lovely thoughts from a very brave lady.

OCTOBER

TUESDAY—OCTOBER 1.

IT was a glorious Autumn morning, with vivid red, gold and yellow leaves still on the trees, and I set off for a stroll. Halfway along the lane I caught up with Harry taking his dog Buffer for a walk. We eventually got round to talking about embarrassing moments in our lives, and he laughed.

Apparently, his nephew who is a theological student had just been to visit him and had told how he'd been sent to preach in an unfamiliar church. He'd had difficulty getting transport, hadn't left himself sufficient time, and was late in arriving.

The service had already started, so he got his breath back, tiptoed quietly up the pulpit steps, and whispered to the minister, "Thank you, I'll carry on from here."

The other man went and sat in the pews and the service continued. When the congregation had departed, the student was making fulsome apologies for his lateness to the minister, then discovered that he was in the wrong church!

WEDNESDAY—OCTOBER 2.

THE teacher of a class of infants held up a pair of gloves and asked, "Whose are these?"

A small boy piped up, "They look like mine, Miss."

"So they are yours, are they, William?"

"No, Miss, they can't be mine, because mine are lost!"

I wonder how many laughs a day our teachers get from children's logic?

THURSDAY—OCTOBER 3.

IN 1913 the Antarctic explorer, Ernest Shackleton, advertised in "The Times": "Men wanted for hazardous journey. Small wages, bitter cold, long months of complete darkness, constant danger, safe return doubtful."

His expedition was to cross the 800-mile Antarctic continent from sea to sea. At one stage Shackleton and two specially-chosen companions had to cross a range of hitherto uncharted mountains rising to 10,000 feet. Night was approaching as they faced yet another steep descent and they had neither the time nor the strength to find another route. Their only alternative was to follow Shackleton's solution of sliding down a rope and plunging into the unknown.

However, it was successful and all returned safely. Later, Shackleton wrote in his book "South": "When I look back on those days, I have no doubt that Providence guided us. I know that during that long and racking march of 36 hours over the unnamed mountains and glaciers of South Georgia, it seemed to me often that we were four, not three. I said nothing to my companions, but afterwards Worsley said to me: 'Boss, I had a curious feeling on the march that there was another person with us.' "

FRIDAY—OCTOBER 4.

THIS delightful verse by Margaret Bentley seems to me to express the very essence of Autumn:

There's Autumn stillness all around,
A crimson carpet on the ground,
But where the leaves lie thick and deep,
The tiny seedlings gently sleep,
Sheltered from wind and bitter rain,
To wake in Spring, and live again.

SATURDAY—OCTOBER 5.

GEORGE BERNARD SHAW once said, "We have no more right to consume happiness without producing it than to consume wealth without producing it."

On a similar theme, G.K. Chesterton wrote, "There are two ways to get enough. One is to continue to accumulate more and more. The other is to desire less and less."

However true, the points being made are likely to be unpopular in much of today's acquisitive society. Nevertheless, whilst I am in a reflective mood, I will add one more quotation, the author of which I cannot now remember: "A contented mind is a continual feast."

SUNDAY—OCTOBER 6.

AND herein do I exercise myself, to have always a conscience void of offence toward God, and toward men. Acts 24:16.

MONDAY—OCTOBER 7.

JEAN HARRIS, of Stockton-On-The-Forest, wrote the following lines. They express a wish I'm sure we all share:

Let me be kind to others,
Forgiving and aware,
Give me the smile, the gentle touch
That show I really care.

Let me know how to listen
And not apportion blame,
And let me be truly thankful
When others do the same.

TUESDAY—OCTOBER 8.

OUR local hall looks wonderful when it is decked out, ready for the annual Autumn Barn Dance.

This year, Mrs Morrison was smiling and working hard at the refreshments counter as usual. However, everything was not quite the same because Betty had lost her only son in a road accident two months before and her beloved husband had died of a heart attack just two weeks later.

During a break in the dancing, I walked over to Betty and said that I hoped that she was as well as could be expected. Her reply was humbling:

"It's been a terrible year," she said, "but I know God has a reason for everything. My prayers always ask him to take care of my loved ones till it is time for me to join them again."

Betty has a serene acceptance of what life, with all its tragedies and traumas, can be if we open our hearts and minds to a higher plane.

WEDNESDAY—OCTOBER 9.

HERE are some thoughts on the theme of "friendship":

Dr Samuel Johnson's advice was "If a man does not make new acquaintances as he advances through life, he will soon find himself alone. A man, Sir, should keep his friendship in constant repair". Whilst Sydney Smith wrote, "Life is to be fortified by many friendships. To love, and be loved, is the greatest happiness of existence".

One of those I like most, though, is in Ecclesiasticus: "A faithful friend is a strong defence: and he that hath found such a one hath found a treasure. A faithful friend is the medicine of life".

So here's a toast to all those who in some way or another "gladden the highways of friendship"!

THURSDAY—OCTOBER 10.

I COULD tell by the glint in young Billy's eye that he had a riddle in store for me.

"Are you feeling good at arithmetic today, Mr Gay?" he asked.

"Oh, yes," I replied, wondering what was coming next.

"Well, how many feet are there in a yard?"

"Three, of course," I said at once.

"Wrong," chuckled Billy. "It all depends how many people are in the yard!"

FRIDAY—OCTOBER 11.

IT'S strange how some stories stay in the mind, isn't it? I remember hearing the tale of a king who had a beautiful and much-cherished daughter. Two rich suitors came to the palace, seeking her hand in marriage.

The king told them that the princess had broken the strap of one of her shoes, and needed a safety pin to make a temporary repair.

One of the young men immediately went in search of a safety pin and then returned to the palace. The other, thinking the request was a trick and that the king would want a son-in-law who would treasure his daughter beyond the gift of a mere pin, went and brought back many rich gifts, including expensive jewels.

Imagine his shock when the king said that he would give the hand of his beloved daughter to the suitor who had brought the pin. "The one who cares for her in little things is the one who really cares," he said.

We may not be able to give expensive gifts to those we love, but we can care for them in many small ways that will have the power to enrich their lives and ours.

ANTICIPATION

Nature doesn't weary us with colour —
Lends it for a day or two, that's all,
Renews her promise of a greener Springtime
With every ochre leaf that starts to fall.

SATURDAY—OCTOBER 12.

THE Lady of the House was in a reminiscent mood about the happy days she had spent as a Girl Guide.

"We had to learn the Guide Promise and Guide Law, Francis, before we could be enrolled," she said, "and I believe I can still remember it. The motto on our hat badge was 'Be Prepared' and the ten parts of the Law included 'A Guide smiles and sings under all difficulties'."

I was most impressed, both with the Lady of the House's excellent memory and with the positive philosophy behind Guiding. Even in the best-regulated household, there's the occasional mishap and then the most helpful attitude is to look on the bright side.

As the old adage tells us, "When you're up to your neck in hot water, be like the kettle and sing."

SUNDAY—OCTOBER 13.

IN my Father's house are many mansions: if it were not so, I would have told you, I go to prepare a place for you.

John 14:2.

MONDAY—OCTOBER 14.

AN unknown poet wrote these lovely lines:

Faith is like a flower
That's in bloom all through the years,
A flower that grows in loveliness
As each new day appears.
And heaven must send its cooling rain
As well as sunny skies,
To make the flower of faith grow strong
And pleasing in His eyes.

TUESDAY—OCTOBER 15.

THE great playwright George Bernard Shaw once observed, "The more you think for yourself, the more marked will your individuality be".

This is certainly true. All have a right to be themselves at the highest level. However, these days when the tendency is to pigeon-hole people, this is sometimes difficult. Yet placing people in categories by saying things such as, "Oh, the old think this . . ." or "The young don't care . . ." causes not merely unhappiness, but real frustration and barriers to understanding.

Margaret Thatcher's father is said to have impressed upon her the importance of not doing something just because others are doing it. "Don't follow the crowd because you're afraid of being different. Decide what you want to do yourself," he told her.

A.J. Rowse, the famous historian, wrote in his book "A Man Of The Thirties":

"My own gospel is that one should fulfil one's inner nature; this way lies creative achievement, not to impose upon one's nature a superstructure not in keeping with it".

That surely means: "Be yourself".

WEDNESDAY—OCTOBER 16.

I CHUCKLED at the story I heard about the little girl who helped her mother in the kitchen because Granny was coming to tea.

"You *have* been a good girl," said Granny as they sat at the table, "and you've iced those buns so smoothly."

"Yes," said the little girl proudly, "that's because I licked them all!"

THURSDAY—OCTOBER 17.

THERE are just 14 lines in this poem by Dorothy M. Loughran, but packed into them is a world of wisdom:

There's always the other side
To the coin,
Life's never so bleak
As it seems;
Turn over the page
And you may find
Fulfilment of your dreams.

It's never the same
On the other side,
There's always a different view;
Opportunity's gate
May be opening wide,
And opening —
Just for you.

FRIDAY—OCTOBER 18.

I HAVE often heard it said, "If you want to be sure something gets done, ask a busy person to do it."

It certainly seems to be true, for it is usually the person who is involved in many things who can be relied on to help out in someone else's emergency. I don't know whether it is a question of temperament — or good organisation!

Whatever it may be it brings its own reward, for I am reminded of another quotation that says, "Happiness is the feeling you get when you're too busy to be miserable".

SATURDAY—OCTOBER 19.

A STRANGER came to live in a small village and was asked to introduce himself. He said, "I never lose my temper, or let others down. I'm always willing to see the other person's point of view and always give freely of my time to help any in need. In fact, I'm a man of complete and utter integrity."

"Never mind," the villagers replied. "We'll still try to like you!"

We wouldn't really like our friends to be perfect, would we? For one thing, what would we have in common with them?

SUNDAY—OCTOBER 20.

FOR I am the Lord that bringeth you up out of the land of Egypt, to be your God: ye shall therefore be holy, for I am holy. Leviticus 11:45.

MONDAY—OCTOBER 21.

OUR local church newsletter included an anonymous poem recently. I don't know where it came from, but I think it's lovely:

The more you give, the more you get,
The more you laugh, the less you fret,
The more you do unselfishly,
The more you live abundantly.
The more of everything you share,
The more you'll always have to spare.
The more you love, the more you'll find
That life is good and friends are kind.
For only what we give away
Enriches us from day to day.

TUESDAY—OCTOBER 22.

A FRIEND'S children take delight in telling me their "Doctor, doctor" jokes. You know the kind of thing . . .

"Doctor, doctor, the invisible man is here!"

"Tell him I can't see him now."

They have an endless supply of such jokes. One I heard contained an interesting little message.

A man went to his doctor. "Doctor, doctor," he said, "nobody likes me."

"Nobody likes you! Why's that?" asked the doctor.

"I haven't the faintest idea, Baldy," the man replied.

A childish joke perhaps, but it gave me a chuckle and made me think. If we use kind words, we're more likely to hear them in reply, aren't we?

WEDNESDAY—OCTOBER 23.

AN acquaintance of ours had a schoolteacher friend staying with her during the recent half-term week. She teaches in one of the inner city schools where she is in charge of a class of six-year-olds.

One day, the children were asked to bring in gifts for the Harvest Festival, so that they could then make up food parcels for the senior citizens in the district.

One little boy from a single-parent family where resources were always very limited, arrived on the appointed day carrying a bowl of cornflakes, which he placed beside the collection of tinned food, cakes, loaves and confectionery.

When his teacher later asked what he had brought, the little boy replied, "Well, Mum said we didn't have anything extra to give away and if I was so keen to give some food I could give my breakfast, so I did."

That little boy's bowl of cereal was worth more than a hamper of food from the richest in the land.

THURSDAY—OCTOBER 24.

IT is sometimes difficult to remember that several of the great preachers of old had a good sense of humour. Charles Haddon Spurgeon, well-known as the People's Preacher at the Metropolitan Tabernacle in London, was once visited by a fellow minister with an unusual type of problem.

Apparently, there was a member of his congregation who used to stuff a finger in each ear at the beginning of his sermon, and sit there with his ears blocked until it was over. What could he, the preacher, do about it?

Spurgeon kept a straight face as he murmured, "I should pray for a fly to alight on his nose."

FRIDAY—OCTOBER 25.

FRIENDS of ours have a magnificent beech tree in their garden. It has stood, increasing in stature, for many years, its Summer leaves giving welcome shade on warm days.

In the Autumn, however, the prickly little beechnuts rain down and Bill and Joan spend hours raking them off the lawn.

How like life that tree is — a mixture of good and bad! Our homes are a great blessing, but sometimes a cause of great worry, too. Our relatives — of course we love them — but aren't they, now and then, just a shade too demanding? Our neighbours — even the best of them can seem unreasonable at times.

Still, let's remember *we* have our faults, too. It's easy to be critical, but next time you feel like complaining or criticising, think of that beech tree and its lovely Summer leaves which more than make up for the beechmast in the Autumn!

SATURDAY—OCTOBER 26.

THERE'S a story about the famous pianist Paderewski who always drew large audiences with his brilliant performances. He was asked for the secret of his success and his reply was: *"Daily practising. If I miss one day, I can tell the difference; if I miss two days, my colleagues know the difference; if I miss three days, my audience knows it, too."*

It's like so many other things in life, isn't it? Perseverance is vital to lasting success.

SUNDAY—OCTOBER 27.

AND immediately there fell from his eyes as it had been scales: and he received sight forthwith, and arose, and was baptised. Acts 9:18.

MONDAY—OCTOBER 28.

BRENDA, who is a nurse, called in to see us recently. She'd lost a fair bit of weight and had also acquired a marvellous tan. She told us she was just back from six months' voluntary work in a Sudanese refugee camp.

A small memento she brought to show us was a hand-made clay doll dressed in strips of bright rag.

"This is a gift I really treasure," she said and then told us about a young woman whom she had nursed back to life from the brink of death. On leaving the camp, the woman wanted to give Brenda some kind of thank-you present, but she had nothing. She then made the clay doll, wrapped it in sacking and presented it to Brenda.

I've noticed before that it's often the simplest gift that turns out to be most cherished.

TUESDAY—OCTOBER 29.

I WAS interested to read this original lesson in anatomy recently.

The body of every organisation is structured from four kinds of bones. There are the wishbones who spend their time wishing someone would do the work. There are the jawbones who do a lot of talking, but little else. There are the knuckle-bones who criticise everything others try to do. Luckily, however, all organisations also have backbones, who carry the load and do the work.

WEDNESDAY—OCTOBER 30.

WOULDN'T life be lots more happy
If the good that's in us all
Were the only thing about us
That folks bothered to recall?

Wouldn't life be lots more happy
If we praised the good we see?
For there's such a lot of goodness
In the worst of you and me.

THURSDAY—OCTOBER 31.

IN 1984 the Rev. Ronald Gallagher set up a world record for the longest sermon. This was delivered in Virginia, in the United States, and it lasted 120 hours. Whether anyone who was there at the beginning was still there at the end, I don't know.

Some of the most memorable sermons are the shortest. One of my favourite mini-sermons is this one on happiness and contentment:

"True happiness lies not in getting what you want, but in wanting what you've got."

FRIDAY—NOVEMBER 1.

A QUIET moment spent in prayer
Refreshes us in mind,
A cleansing of the spirit's needs
Can help us all to find
That precious strength of will to cope
With all the day may bring,
For if we have life's inner strength,
We have life's everything.

Elizabeth Gozney.

SATURDAY—NOVEMBER 2.

THERE are probably lots of people reading this book who would like to be a millionaire, if only for a day or two.

Quite a lot of rich men, however, miss life's treasures simply because making lots of money can be a full-time occupation. It's often a case of all work and no play. Everyone needs time for recreation and reflection — even millionaires.

Next time you are tempted to overwork or wish you had vast amounts of money at your disposal, think of these words carved some 200 years ago on a stone in a quiet country churchyard. They contain so much good, sound commonsense:

If your nose is close to the grindstone,
And you keep it there long enough,
In time you'll say there's no such thing
As brooks that babble and birds that sing.
These three things will all your world compose,
Just you, the stone and your poor old nose.

SUNDAY—NOVEMBER 3.

AS for me, behold, I am in your hand; do with me as seemeth good and meet unto you.

Jeremiah 26:14.

MONDAY—NOVEMBER 4.

COMPUTERS, space travel, television that brings the world into our homes at the touch of a button . . . there are so many modern wonders that there seems little left to surprise us. However, Andy Rooney, an American writer, found something when thinking of the exhilaration of a warm shower first thing in the morning.

"I like the warmth and I like the idea that I am part of a civilisation that has organised itself to get water to my house and have it warm and waiting for me when I get up. It's difficult to remember to be amazed every day, but it *is* amazing!"

TUESDAY—NOVEMBER 5.

WHAT a dull, drab day," I thought as I walked along the High Street. The sky was grey, the rain was pouring down and the shoppers hurrying about their business all seemed to be clad in sombre hues of blacks, browns and navy blues.

There was nothing cheerful in sight — until I spotted the Lady of the House waiting underneath her bright red umbrella at the place we had arranged to meet. With a welcoming smile, she took my arm and drew me into the little tea-shop for an afternoon cup of tea.

What a difference that spot of colour and the sight of a loved face made to my day! Such a meeting can brighten up any situation.

WEDNESDAY—NOVEMBER 6.

IT was Oscar Wilde who wrote, "There is only one thing in the world worse than being talked about and that is not being talked about."

Nobody enjoys being gossiped about, criticised or having their faults pointed out, and all these things can cause a great deal of pain. But it is even worse if the good things in a person are ignored — their kindness, talents and achievements, their patience and dignity in trouble or suffering. These, I believe, are all things worth talking about. Let's try to do it more often!

THURSDAY—NOVEMBER 7.

BETH has been house-bound for some years now, but as she says, it's only her body that can't travel. Her mind is still free and she can "travel" in memory to the loveliest places. Last time I visited Beth, she told me that one of her favourite pastimes is to recall rooms she has known.

Her first room, after she left home, was high up in the eaves of a large, rambling house. Her bed was under a sloping ceiling, and at night the little attic window made a gateway to the stars.

Another room in Beth's memory bank is the country kitchen when she was a new bride. There was a dresser laden with willow-pattern china, and a black cooking range where the kettle sang continuously to welcome friends.

Have you a special room you remember from long ago? I have. It was crammed with books and an old leather armchair. There was a small writing table where someone once placed fresh snowdrops on St Valentine's Day . . .

But that's another story.

THE WAY AHEAD

FRIDAY—NOVEMBER 8.

I SAW these words on a Wayside Pulpit recently: "Tis far better to forgive and forget than to resent and remember. Love reduces friction to a fraction".

It does, too!

SATURDAY—NOVEMBER 9.

TODAY we remember those who died in two World Wars.

It was Colonel John McCrae whose poem "In Flanders Fields" made the poppy a symbol of remembrance, but it is perhaps not so well-known that an American lady, Moina Michael, wrote some moving lines in reply:

We cherish, too, the poppy red
That grows on fields where valour led,
It seems to signal to the skies
That blood of heroes never dies . . .

Just before the Armistice was signed, she bought 25 poppies, wore one herself and sold the others to 24 of her colleagues — probably the first organised selling of poppies.

Now, disabled ex-servicemen make the artificial poppies and their sale makes it possible to give help in time of need to those who lost so much for the sake of their country. Today, as in every year since 1921, millions of poppies will be worn to keep faith with those who lost their lives — and I, too, shall wear mine with pride.

SUNDAY—NOVEMBER 10.

STRENGTHEN ye the weak hands, and confirm the feeble knees. Isaiah 35:3.

MONDAY—NOVEMBER 11.

DO you know what the word sterling means? It refers both to impeccable character and good money. The word itself originates from the early Middle Ages, when most of the shipping of Europe was carried on by traders and merchants from the Baltic area and Eastern Europe. Known as the Hanseatic League, because they came from Eastern Europe, they were sometimes called "Easterlings", too. They brought their goods to England and Scotland, and exported British wool, cloth, and corn to the Continent.

In order to trade, some kind of money was needed, and the British made money specially for the Easterlings. Because they were honest traders, the money they used was always valued because folk knew it would be honoured, and they would always get their money's worth of goods.

The Easterlings' money was named after them, and in the course of time the first two letters were dropped. That is how our currency came to be known as sterling.

Sterling still has a good name, and it doesn't only refer to money. Sterling friends are worth their weight in anybody's coin, aren't they?

TUESDAY—NOVEMBER 12.

DO a little kindness,
Any sort will do;
Sure as life's worth living
It comes back to you,
Warms your heart and makes you
Happy as can be;
If you don't believe it,
Just try it and see!

WEDNESDAY—NOVEMBER 13.

FOUR-YEAR-OLD Sarah was playing in her room when, from the kitchen, she heard her mother singing — rather badly, it has to be said.

Sarah put up with it for a time, but at last she called out, "Mummy, you're singing in the wrong direction!"

THURSDAY—NOVEMBER 14.

ONCE, Athene Syler, the actress, was speaking on the radio about her life and career. She told listeners that she went to church whenever she could and that one of her favourite hymns was "Morning Has Broken":

Morning has broken
Like the first morning;
Blackbird has spoken
Like the first bird.
Praise for the singing,
Praise for the morning,
Praise for them, springing
Fresh from the Word!

"I alter the words when I sing it," said Athene. "I sit near to the choir, and I can see them smiling at me as I sing:

Morning has broken,
Pick up the pieces,
Pick up the pieces
All the day long!"

Eleanor Farjeon, the writer of the hymn, knew that, on a lovely sunny Summer morning when the birds are singing, we feel complete and at peace. But we all know that peace can all too often be shattered — life is not like a Summer day any longer. It's then that we have to pick up the pieces, with Athene Syler.

FRIDAY—NOVEMBER 15.

EARLY one morning, the Scottish poet Edward B. Ramsay listened to a blackbird singing on a tree outside his home. Then he sat down and penned these lines:

O that my soul could sing like this,
And know the perfect joy and bliss
Of morning and of evening praise,
In thankfulness for God's good ways;
And though my heart were still aware
Of every sorrow, every care,
Each one would soar to Heaven above,
Lost in the harmony of love.

SATURDAY—NOVEMBER 16.

SOMEBODY with a very demanding job was asked on television what she did when she wanted to recharge her batteries.

"Well," she said, "I have a country cottage and I go there and put a "Keep Out" notice on the door. There I enjoy the peace and quietness of the countryside, I have time to walk and think, and then I come back to work in a better frame of mind."

We may not all have a country cottage to retreat to, but we can shut out the world and find mental refreshment in so many ways — in music or a good book, in a garden, a walk in the park or a cup of tea with a friend. I'm sure we could all make our own list of "places of peace".

SUNDAY—NOVEMBER 17.

GOD is a spirit: and they that worship him must worship him in spirit and in truth. John 4:24.

MONDAY—NOVEMBER 18.

THE Lady of the House was excited at the prospect of meeting an old schoolfriend again. They hadn't met since Madge's marriage and departure for America many years ago, and now she was to spend a few days of reunion with us.

There was much laughter as they pored over old class photographs of gym-slipped girls, picking out individuals and reminiscing over happy — and not so happy — times. I must admit I escaped to the greenhouse on several occasions!

"It was lovely to see Madge again," remarked the Lady of the House when the visit was over, "and the strange thing was that although it's so many years since we saw each other, we just picked up the threads where we had left off."

"That's not at all surprising," I said, and I reminded her of the lines:

Links of gold may dull and sever,
But links of friendship last forever.

TUESDAY—NOVEMBER 19.

MANY people think that nuns are completely free from the problems, temptations and irritations that we lesser mortals have to face, so I was interested to hear something that a Mother Superior said to a new nun when she received her into the Order:

"Remember, you have not chosen your Sisters, nor in the most part would you have done so."

What wise words these are! Fortunately, in this country we are able to choose our marriage partners and also our friends, but many things are decided for us — our place of birth, our teachers and class mates, our neighbours and colleagues at work. Learning to get along with people and to like what is good in them is one of the great lessons of life.

WEDNESDAY—NOVEMBER 20.

RECENTLY I watched a television programme in which a gardener talked about his enthusiasm for raising alpine plants for his rockery. He demonstrated the planting of seeds in small pots, the watering and then the laying aside in a cool atmosphere until germination took place.

"All you can do then," he said, "is wait. They may take twelve months, or even two, three or four years before there is any sign of growth, but never give up hope."

There's a good lesson for life here. As with so many things, for instance bringing up children, training an animal, learning a new craft or building a relationship, hurrying does no good and the only way to make real progress is with care and patience.

THURSDAY—NOVEMBER 21.

ONE of the things I look forward to is the television presentation of the Leeds International Pianoforte Competition which takes place every three years. Along with many others I always try to pick the winner.

I remember Fanny Waterman, the founder and one of the judges, being asked how she was able to judge between performers when, technically, there was so little difference. Her reply was, "I need to have my emotions touched. When a performance moves me to tears I know I have had a good day."

This emotion that can lift a performance from the good to the truly great can lead to a deeper understanding. I am reminded of the old lady who said, "It's nice to have a laugh together sometimes, but to be real friends, folk have to weep together."

Wise words.

FRIDAY—NOVEMBER 22.

I LIKED this description of a grandmother by an eight-year-old which was printed in the magazine of the Mothers' Union:

"A grandmother is a lady who has no children of her own, so she likes other people's little girls and boys. Grandmothers don't have to do anything but be there. They are old, so they shouldn't play hard or run. They should never say 'Hurry up'. Usually they are fat, but not too fat to tie children's shoes. They don't have to be smart, only answer questions like why cats hate dogs and why God isn't married. They don't make baby-talk like visitors. When they read to us, they don't skip bits, or mind if it is the same story over again. Everybody should have one, especially if you don't have television, because grandmothers are the only grown-ups who have time to spare".

SATURDAY—NOVEMBER 23.

IN my old Bible there is a picture illustrating St Paul's plea to "Bear ye one another's burdens". It shows a line of pilgrims walking along the road, each with a pack on his back, and each supporting the pack on the back of the person in front.

It's a lovely example of the help we give and receive throughout life — and very often, just at the time we are giving somebody a helping hand with a burden, we find our own is being lifted, too.

SUNDAY—NOVEMBER 24.

KEEP yourselves in the love of God, looking for the mercy of our Lord Jesus Christ unto eternal life.

Jude 1:21.

MONDAY—NOVEMBER 25.

CHILDREN bring a freshness to many things—even their prayers, as I discovered from this one in a church magazine:

For sausages, baked beans and crisps,
For papers full of fish and chips,
For ice-cream full of chocolate bits,
Thanks, God.

For furry caterpillars to keep,
For woodlice with their tickly feet,
For crabs we catch with bits of meat,
Thanks, God.

For bicycles and roller skates,
For playing football with my mates,
For times when I can stay up late,
Thanks, God.

TUESDAY—NOVEMBER 26.

HAVE you heard of the asparagus test?

I hadn't until the other day when the Lady of the House served one of my favourite soups — asparagus. When I told her how good it was, she said, "I was given the recipe by that Dutch lady, Brigette, who's just come to stay here.

"She was telling me that at her church at home, they had a new minister and everybody was pleased to see that he had started to grow asparagus in his garden."

"What was so good about that?" I asked.

"That's what I wondered, too. But it's quite simple. Brigette explained that it takes three years to get a crop from asparagus so, when a minister starts growing it, it means he won't be in a hurry to leave!"

FASCINATION

WEDNESDAY—NOVEMBER 27.

WHEN Betty retired after many years of working as a hairdresser in a local salon, she received many gifts and well-deserved compliments. A number of customers when booking appointments had particularly asked for Betty to do their hair. It was said that she had an artistic flair and that her customers always left the salon looking much better than when they came in.

The nicest compliment she received, however, took her by surprise. "I never left Betty without *feeling* good," one regular customer said. "And not just because my well-groomed hair gave me a boost, but because of the kind of person Betty is. She always has time for me, makes me feel worthwhile, and is interested in me as a person. Somehow she makes a visit to the hairdresser's fun."

These are sterling qualities, not only for a hairdresser, but for all of us, whatever our calling in life.

THURSDAY—NOVEMBER 28.

LITTLE Stephen's seventh birthday was approaching and his parents asked him what he would like as a present. He said he would like a bicycle, but on consideration, his parents decided a tricycle would be safer.

When Stephen's birthday arrived, his parents made sure they were hiding where they could see his reaction when he saw his present.

His reaction, however, was somewhat unexpected. Lifting up his eyes to Heaven, he exclaimed, "Oh God, I thought you knew the difference between a bicycle and a tricycle!"

FRIDAY—NOVEMBER 29.

IN a society where we are more likely to hear about the bad things rather than the good, it is always good to learn of a generous action.

I heard recently about a little girl who was found sobbing in a supermarket in a very deprived area where there was a high level of unemployment. She was crying because she had lost the £10 note she had been given to do the shopping.

In a matter of minutes, the customers had organised a whip-round to replace the money, somebody helped her to do the shopping and someone else saw her safely home.

It's one of those incidents that prove that it is often the poorest of people who are ready to share the little they have — just as it is often those who have suffered personal grief who know how to give a helping hand to others.

SATURDAY—NOVEMBER 30.

DR DALE, the great Victorian preacher, told a story about a lady who had stopped him in a Birmingham street. "God bless you, Dr Dale," she said. She refused to give her name but just thanked him for a helpful message he had given in a sermon and then went on her way.

It so happened that Dr Dale had been feeling very depressed. "But," he said, "as soon as she spoke to me, the mist broke, the sunlight came; I breathed the free air of the mountains of God."

It often needs only a few thoughtful words to lift someone from the shadow of unhappiness. How we appreciate it when this happens to us — and isn't it nice for us to have the satisfaction of knowing we have helped someone else?

SUNDAY—DECEMBER 1.

AND the angel said unto them, Fear not: for, behold, I bring you good tidings of great joy, which shall be to all people. Luke 2:10.

MONDAY—DECEMBER 2.

THE REV. W. AWDRY told his small son stories about a little engine called Edward. He later scribbled them down on the backs of old circulars. One day, his wife found these crumpled scraps of paper, read them — and from there, they ended up on a publisher's desk!

In a television interview some years ago, Awdry told how he was always known as "the Thomas the Tank Engine Man". He liked this, he said, because it showed that thousands of children loved his characters. Indeed, he received numerous scrawly letters and wobbly drawings of Thomas from young enthusiasts.

Thomas and his friends have real personalities and get into lots of mischief, too. Their creator's philosophy about the stories was: "This is God's world, you can obey Him or disobey Him. The engines, like us humans, often go their own way and inevitably come to a sticky end. The point is, they are punished but never scrapped!"

When I read one of the stories to a young friend, I found Thomas saying, "There is always another opportunity to try harder to become a really useful engine — and to get there."

One of the many clever little sermons Thomas has preached!

TUESDAY—DECEMBER 3.

DECEMBER can seem rather a bleak month at the start, with its cold winds, short days and frequently black skies. But then a wonderful change takes place, and we begin to notice things we didn't see before. There are bright scarlet berries where we once thought the twigs were barren. There are amazing, intricate lace patterns on the frosty boughs. There's a smile on our neighbours' faces, and later perhaps, the unexpected arrival of a Christmas card from a long-lost friend.

Suddenly, we feel better. It is as if the light of Christmas helps us to see more clearly. When candles are lit and carols are sung, we cannot help but feel our hearts warmed by love. Isn't it true, that the joyful sight of the new baby in the manger can rekindle hope for the future?

WEDNESDAY—DECEMBER 4.

ALTHOUGH Annie's son, Matthew, is now in his twenties and living away from home, he still goes back home when a word of timely advice is needed.

I met Annie last week. She was standing at her garden gate, saying goodbye to Matthew after he'd called unexpectedly.

As Matthew got on his motor-bike, I heard him say, "Thanks, Mum! I knew you'd have the right answer because you've been through all this yourself."

As Annie has had more than her fair share of life's troubles, it was easy to understand her wry smile as Matthew drove off.

I could not help but be reminded of the words of that wise man John Bunyan, "Though with great difficulty I got here, yet now I do not regret all the trouble I have been in to arrive where I am."

THURSDAY—DECEMBER 5.

THE same time every morning
Sees the post land on our mat,
I always rush to see it
When I hear "rat-a-tat-tat!"
There may be news from relatives
Who are far across the sea,
Perhaps an invitation
To meet a friend for tea.
Reminders and leaflets
Can bring frowns or smiles,
Postmarks sometimes puzzle:
Where are these unknown isles?
Pretty picture postcards
Say "Wish you were here",
A grand-daughter writes
To a grandma who's dear.
The postman brings a lot of joy
— Very rarely sorrow
He may pass by this morning,
But he'll be back tomorrow!

Barbara Jemison.

FRIDAY—DECEMBER 6.

MY friend George is a minister and he felt rather pleased when a member of his congregation came up to him after morning service and said, "Your sermons always remind me of the peace and mercy of God."

It wasn't until George got home that he remembered that the peace of God passes all understanding, and His mercy endureth forever.

He still isn't sure whether he was given a compliment or not!

SATURDAY—DECEMBER 7.

AT the age of eight, Peter had already got certain things clear in his mind regarding generosity.

Sorting out toys for the Sunday School Christmas Gift Service, he put aside some little cars, a few jig-saws, and one or two picture-books. His mother, looking them over, was surprised to see, sitting beside them, his favourite toy dog.

"Is Bonzo going, too?" she asked amazed.

Peter pointed to the pile of gifts. "I'm giving away these," he explained. Then, indicating his well-loved Bonzo, he added, "But I'm *giving* him."

SUNDAY—DECEMBER 8.

HE loveth righteousness and judgement: the earth is full of the goodness of the Lord. Psalms 33:5.

MONDAY—DECEMBER 9.

A YOUNG man had been appointed as organist at a chapel in one of the moorland villages of Yorkshire. He was anxious to make a good impression when he accompanied the augmented choir in its annual rendering of Handel's "Messiah", and no trill or ornamentation was left out.

All went well, with the organ-blower pumping away, until the final chorus — and then, suddenly, the sound faded away.

"What's wrong?" whispered the organist. "We haven't finished yet."

"Nay, lad," replied the organ-blower, "It only takes 300 pumps for the 'Messiah' and you've had that. I'm off home now."

JOY OF WINTER

TUESDAY—DECEMBER 10.

"IT'S December," said the Lady of the House, "and I have just seen my first bit of cheerfulness since the Spring." She didn't mean it literally, of course; she was referring to a bunch of "cheerfulness", that bright little flower of the narcissus family, which had caught her eye in a friend's house.

And how good it is to see these reminders of Spring in the darkest days of Winter — the hyacinths we planted in the Autumn, poking through the fibre in the bowls, the birdsong on a bright morning, and the days slowly, and at first imperceptibly, lengthening. It won't be long before we can echo Shelley's words:

And the Spring arose on the garden fair,
Like the Spirit of Love felt everywhere.

WEDNESDAY—DECEMBER 11.

RECENTLY I had the pleasure of accompanying a young friend who was competing in a local drama festival. During the interval, a group of us were discussing the Original Poem Class over a cup of tea. One of the contestants said that writing poetry came very easily to her. In fact, she confessed that if somebody upset her or made her very annoyed, she would straight away write down her feelings in verse — and then the next day, having got it off her chest, she would tear up her work and feel a lot better.

Well, we may not all be able to write poetry, but it does seem a good idea, instead of bearing resentment, to get rid of any bad feelings by putting them in writing and then destroying them and being done with them forever. I can't remember who it was that said "You get bitter — or you get better", but how true it is!

THURSDAY—DECEMBER 12.

WHEN a newly-ordained vicar arrived in his first parish, he found that there was opposition to some of the small changes he was proposing. His clergy friends told him that this was not uncommon.

One day he decided to visit his oldest parishioner, a 96-year-old lady, much loved in the district. He felt that if he could win her support, his improvements would be accepted more willingly. On the way to her cottage, he had what he thought was a good idea. "I'll tell her that change is inevitable. After all, when the previous vicar retired it *was* inevitable that there would be a new one."

He remarked on this to the old lady and she said nothing. Confidently he pressed on, "I expect that in your long association with the parish, you have seen many changes."

"Aye," the old lady replied, "and I've opposed them all!"

FRIDAY—DECEMBER 13.

MOST of us know the story of the wise men and their gifts of gold, frankincense and myrrh, symbolising kingship, priesthood and sacrifice. But there are legends based on other gifts brought in adoration to the manger.

There is a charming one about a little girl who followed the shepherds on their journey to Bethlehem. Everyone had a gift to present to the Christ Child except the little girl, and she was very sad because she had nothing to offer.

As she lingered behind, an angel appeared, scattering beautiful white roses along the way. Gladly the little girl picked them up, and ran to the stable and laid them at the feet of the little Lord Jesus. They were the very first Christmas roses.

SATURDAY—DECEMBER 14.

A REGULAR reader of "The Friendship Book", Mrs Dorothy M. Weaving, wrote to tell me of an experience she had many years ago when she had been going through a period of great anxiety.

"At the time," she writes, "I was not a Christian, and I cannot even remember what was worrying me so much. I was in my first year of training for nursing and working on a ward with quite seriously ill patients. This dear gentleman must have seen how worried I was. He took my hands in his and said these beautiful words which he made me promise never to forget:

"Fear knocked at the door.
Faith answered.
There was no-one there.

"I never did forget. They are on the fly-leaf of my Bible and they have often given me great comfort."

Nearly all our fears, if faced head on, lose their terror. Let us today remember with gratitude the thoughtful concern of friends who point us in the right direction — and the love for us from which that concern springs.

SUNDAY—DECEMBER 15.

FOR the grace of God that bringeth salvation hath appeared to all men. Titus 2:11.

MONDAY—DECEMBER 16.

I MUST confess I am not very familiar with the writings of Leo Aikman, but I cherish these lines of his which I came on some years ago:

"Blessed is the person who is too busy to worry in the daytime and too sleepy to worry at night."

TUESDAY—DECEMBER 17.

ONE 17th of December, an 11-year-old boy in a blue flannel shirt and jeans could be seen going into a jeweller's shop. He was paying the last instalment on a necklace and earrings for his mother's Christmas present.

Well, there's nothing remarkable about that, you might think. However, the boy's mother had seen them the previous Easter, and couldn't afford them, so her son had been paying for them gradually for eight whole months. That December day, the boy had walked all the way to the jeweller's shop because he needed what would have been the bus fare for the journey to pay the last payment.

Beginning as early as Easter, he had denied himself his own wants in order to buy his widowed mother a Christmas present she really wanted. That 11-year-old's loving little heart knew a lot about the sacrifices of love.

WEDNESDAY—DECEMBER 18.

WINIFRED HOLTBY, the talented Yorkshire writer, was only 37 when she died in 1935. Her best-known novel is "South Riding", an autobiographical tale of life in a small Yorkshire town in the years between the Wars, and she is remembered as a keen idealist who was passionately in love with everything good.

The inscription on her tombstone in Rudston churchyard, in the Yorkshire Wolds, reads:

God give me work
Till my life shall end,
And life
Till my work is done.

All of us might wish for the same.

SMALL TALK

Hello — who's there?
I've come here to call,
I can't come in
'Cos I'm much too tall.

THURSDAY—DECEMBER 19.

WHEN the famous film director, Franco Zeffirelli, made his television film about Jesus, he assembled a cast which included many of the greatest actors and actresses of the time.

Some wondered how they would get on working together on a film set. After all, each one was used to being *the* star of the film. Zeffirelli, however, had a message for them. "In this film," he said, "there will be only one star — the Star of Bethlehem."

Each Christmas we remember the Bethlehem Star as the one that leads us to the real meaning of Christmas.

FRIDAY—DECEMBER 20.

A DISABLED man wrote down these thoughts which I repeat here, hoping they will help us all to be more understanding:

"Blessed are you who walk with us in public places and ignore the stares of strangers, for in your companionship we find havens of relaxation.

"Blessed are you who never bid us to 'hurry up' and, more blessed, you who do not snatch our tasks from us, for often we need time rather than help.

"Blessed are you who take time to listen to difficult speech, for you help us to know that if we persevere we can be understood.

"Blessed are you who stand beside us when we enter new and untried ventures, for our failure will be outweighed by the times when we surprise ourselves and you.

"Blessed are you who ask for help, for our greatest need is to be needed.

"Rejoice and be exceedingly glad, for you deal with us as God has dealt with all His children".

SATURDAY—DECEMBER 21.

I LIKE these verses by the Winchester poet, Dorothy M. Loughran:

Just for today, with willing heart
I'll do my best to play my part,
Try not to grumble, or to boast,
Get on with things that I hate most.

Just for today, and all day long,
I'll try and put right what is wrong,
Why just today? With added zest
I'll try each day to do my best.

SUNDAY—DECEMBER 22.

AND when they were come into the house, they saw the young child with Mary his mother, and fell down, and worshipped him: and when they had opened their treasures, they presented unto him gifts; gold, and frankincense and myrrh. Matthew 2:11.

MONDAY—DECEMBER 23.

BISHOP Phillips Brooks, the genial 19th-century giant of the American pulpit, is perhaps best known for his Christmas hymn, "O little town of Bethlehem."

But he was also a fine preacher, with the gift of putting into simple language the most profound thoughts. In one of his sermons he was speaking about faith, and he remarked that the cleverest man could find no better way of understanding what belief in Christ is than by ticking off upon his fingers, as a child might, the five letters of the word FAITH and saying, "Forsaking All I Take Him".

TUESDAY—DECEMBER 24.

WE all know the saying, "It pays to advertise," even, it seems, when we're as young as Tommy and his brother, Peter. They were being put to bed by their grandma who had come to stay with the family for Christmas.

While they were undressing, Grandma popped into the bathroom to tidy up after them.

They knelt to say their prayers and Tommy ended up in a loud voice with a request for a pair of roller skates for Christmas.

"Not so loud," said Peter. "God isn't deaf."

"No, of course not," replied Tommy, "but Grandma is."

WEDNESDAY—DECEMBER 25.

AT a carol service a few years ago, I copied down from the service paper this closing prayer:

"When the Christmas candles are burned out, the carols have died away, the star is set, all the radiant song-filled night has passed, Thou alone, the Eternal, remainest, and Thou art enough. Remain in us, more beautiful, more beloved, more real than any of the romance that clusters round Thy birthday."

THURSDAY—DECEMBER 26.

ONE Boxing Day, Daniel, aged nearly four, picked up his Grandad's newly-acquired camera and wanted to take a picture with it. Grandad, not too surprisingly, removed his precious Christmas present to a safer spot.

Daniel protested with the impeccable logic of experience, "But Grandpa, you must learn to share your toys!"

THE CALL OF CHRISTMAS

FRIDAY—DECEMBER 27.

WE are constantly reminded that Britain has an ageing population. Is this a bad thing? There may be argument about that, but there's no doubting how useful older folk can be.

As we advance in years, we tend to enjoy recalling events of the past — perhaps how the Coronation, Jubilees and other national events were celebrated in our village, town or city. Then there are memories of schooldays, the pleasure, for example, of returning home from school on Winter afternoons to the warmth of a large coal fire and the delicious smell of baked apples being cooked for tea in the side oven of the kitchen range.

No longer are such memories regarded as trivial and boring. In fact, they are very important. Some older people have been encouraged to write their life stories after attending local history and other interest groups. Others merely sit and talk of the past, while members of local oral history teams tape their reminiscences. Such memories are invaluable to the local history classes now flourishing in many places.

Yes, older people have a lot to contribute — just because they're old!

SATURDAY—DECEMBER 28.

WHEN the vicar of a South London parish was leaving his flock to take up a charge in the Midlands, he wrote to several removal firms asking for quotations.

One company replied saying that they were very experienced when it came to the contents of vicarages. The letter continued: "In the past three years we have removed 20 clergymen to the satisfaction of all concerned."

SUNDAY—DECEMBER 29.

BARBARA JEMISON, the Bridlington poet, sent me this verse from an old family autograph album:

The road's uphill for you, but sure
You'll reach the top at length.
The way is steep and rough, but friend,
You'll find the needed strength.
So climb and sing and pray and strive
In spite of thorn and stone,
For if God be your guide, why then,
You do not climb alone.

MONDAY—DECEMBER 30.

NOW unto the King eternal, immortal, invisible, the only wise God, be honour and glory for ever and ever. Amen. Timothy I 1:17.

TUESDAY—DECEMBER 31.

A FRIEND from Hamburg, the city that suffered so much damage in World War II, has been telling me about a lovely New Year custom there.

As midnight on New Year's Eve approaches, the city remains in darkness, but children are waiting on the balconies of their homes or public buildings. As the clocks begin to strike the hour, the children's sparklers are lit, one held in each hand, and as they wave them round in circles, the city bursts into light.

It seems very appropriate that, as the old year dies, it is the youngsters with their fresh hope and enthusiasm who symbolise the light and life of another year.

A very happy New Year to everyone!

Where The Photographs Were Taken

PEAK PERFORMANCE — *Loch Ard and Ben Lomond.*
THE GLORY OF STONE — *Gloucester Cathedral.*
WHITE MORNING — *Eardisland, Herefordshire.*
GOLD AND GREEN — *The River Exe, Bickleigh, Devon.*
REFLECTIONS — *Leeds Castle, Kent.*
PEACEFUL PATH — *Epping Forest.*
FRIENDS ALONG THE WAY — *Watendlath Bridge, Cumbria.*
LOOKING FORWARD — *The West Highland Way, Milngavie.*
SAFE HAVEN — *Brixham Harbour, Devon.*
MASTER CRAFTSMAN — *Wytham, Oxfordshire.*
CRUISING BY — *The Thames at Clifton Hampden.*
OLD FAVOURITES — *Weymouth Beach.*
MELLOW THOUGHTS — *Childrey Village Pond, Wantage, Oxfordshire.*
NATURE'S PATTERNS — *Naunton, Gloucestershire.*
AUTUMN EASE — *The River Ouse, York.*
HEAVEN SENT — *Plockton, Wester Ross.*
ANTICIPATION — *Halstead, Essex.*
JOY OF WINTER — *Knaresborough Castle, Yorkshire.*
THE CALL OF CHRISTMAS — *Bath Abbey.*

Printed and Published by D. C. THOMSON & CO., LTD., 185 Fleet Street, London EC4A 2HS.

ISBN 0-85116-490-0